C-FACTORS
THE SECRET 36

ARE YOU MISSING THE BLUEPRINT?

SUNDAR KUMARASAMY

C-Factors: The Secret 36
Are You Missing the Blueprint?

Copyright © Sundar Kumarasamy (2025)

ISBN Paperback: 979-8-89576-130-4

Published by:

Table of Contents

The Tides of Change

I have spent well over twenty-five years studying and creating ways to improve students' enrollment and journey through several colleges worldwide. During these decades of actively impacting the lives of young students and experienced professionals, one thing has become quite clear to me: the world is changing fast, and we need to focus on providing equitable access to resources and structures that will improve learning and teach humanity to embrace change. One way to boost human behaviour through learning is by creating experiential opportunities that cultivate skills essential for success in the modern professional landscape. In navigating the tide of change, this is the first point of call.

The Power of 'C': Unlocking Your Potential

I am not a believer in the concept of time travel, but the idea of having an opportunity to travel to the past and future has always seemed exciting to me. Not particularly because I desire to invest in stocks and become one of the world's wealthiest persons, nor because I would like to have a look at the partner I was destined to spend life with, and save myself from some painful heartbreaks! No, I find the notion of time travel appealing because it would allow humanity to right its wrongs before they happen, prepare for the future with all the necessary tools, and learn the traits and habits necessary to improve their lives. I believe that this knowledge of what to consume and what to avoid would go a long way in helping young people get a grip on their lives.

However, we have to face reality. There is currently no way any human being can rectify the past or know the future. When we look back on our lives, we have no way of knowing how they'll turn out or if we will emerge as winners or losers. The only thing we can do is try our very best to create a future of happiness and fulfillment for ourselves. This much is within our control.

There are errors to avoid, mistakes to correct, and bad habits to root out of our lives - these are practical ways to design the future we desire. While we wait for the scientific community to crack the possibility of time travel, I have explored the possibility of the next best thing - experiences and projections. I have spoken to diverse people with rich life experiences, conducted several research studies into the psychology of human nature, and collated stories from the past to help predict the future. In this book, I have made recommendations that will help every reader maximize their potential and strive for excellence.

Why Words Shape Our Reality

Firstly, there's something that has resonated in my research, discussions, and experiences. It is that we are not as powerless to determine our future as we often think we are. Humans have an uncanny ability to change. And change is the most powerful force in determining the waves of our destiny. However, we do not often realize the power we wield, so we allow life to happen *to* us instead of taking charge of our words, thoughts, and actions to determine the kind of life we *want*. However, do we understand the power of our words in shaping our reality? Do we understand how much our words have to do with the attitude we have towards life? Do we fully understand how much effect the things we say have on us?

The Science Behind Linguistic Priming

Research has revealed that the way we think and talk about a situation can greatly influence our brain's reaction to it. It is a phenomenon called "Linguistic Priming." I have utilized this science to teach my brain how to react in various situations. For example, when I am faced with a challenging task, I use words that influence my thoughts to see what is before me as an opportunity to learn and grow. The effect of this is that instead of being afraid of the task and entertaining doubts and fears, my brain is pumped up for the challenge. It doesn't make the task itself any easier, but I often find that I certainly enjoy it more.

Navigating the 6x6 Matrix: A New Framework for Holistic Growth

To help my readers understand how they can create a culture of change to bring about personal transformation, I have put together a 6 by 6 matrix that, when followed, will lead to **all-around** holistic growth. These six 'C' words interact across key dimensions of life—self, relationships, career, health, mindset, and community, and show how positive change and growth can be achieved. The pillars—Character, Creativity, Communication, Change, Completion, and Connection—are building blocks that drive progress, but the magic happens when they work together.

The Butterfly Effect in Personal Development

Every major transformation begins with a small act—one question, one conversation, one decision. I call it the *butterfly effect*. The butterfly effect is a seemingly insignificant step that triggers far-reaching consequences. We often ignore small steps because they do not seem all that impressive, but if we want to grow, we must learn to stack each small achievement on top of the other and take one step at a time. The 6 by 6 matrix is the perfect compass for this, as it guides you on each step and shows you how they can be applied in real life.

How Each 'C' Word Builds Upon the Others

Each chapter includes actionable lessons that will help you reflect, plan, and act. You will discover frameworks to apply immediately, because transformation doesn't happen in theory; it always happens in practice. I recommend reading this book as a process of steady growth from where you are to where you want to be. This builds ease and progress as you grow in a step-wise order. I hope this book changes you and opens your eyes to the possibilities that lie before you when you take initiative.

Your Sea Change Journey: From Ripples to the biggest oceans and longest rivers all started with just a single drop. Those drops turned into ripples, the ripples built into waves, and eventually, they came together to form the oceans and rivers we know. We usually notice the waves, not the little drops or gentle ripples that came first. But think about it—can you have a sea without the tiny drops that made it? That's what this book is all about—the small steps, the little changes, the daily habits that add up over time. Each chapter is like a drop, and together they help you build the kind of mindset that can shift your life.

Small Steps, Monumental Impact

Nothing great happens overnight; we gather momentum for greatness through intentional, carefully planned action steps that accumulate to make a big impact. This book has been written to be a daily step-by-step improvement tool for you to reflect and make a conscious effort to change. The intentional arrangement of the chapters and subheadings will also help you to easily internalize the concepts until you realize, probably a full year later, that things have changed for the better for you.

What You Can Expect from This Book

This book provides a roadmap to personal and professional transformation. It's a collection of ideas, stories, recommendations, and solutions to societal, professional, and personal challenges recorded by humanity throughout history. Every page provides a sequence of deliberate decisions and action points that will inch you toward the best version of yourself. If you want to attain quantifiable excellence in your personal and professional life, then I implore you to study each chapter intentionally.

Practical Exercises and Real-World Applications

I have shared my personal stories and strategies I employed throughout my career to help bring more practicality and reality into the book. As you read, you may find yourself resonating with several stories and illustrations that happened to me in my early years as a professional. Whether you want to use the principles of this book in your day-to-day interactions, in your professional career, or in improving your relationships, you will find tips that will help you inculcate the positive qualities represented throughout the chapters.

Global Perspectives and Universal Principles

While this book has been written from a personal perspective to help its readers relate and sympathize more with the ideas, I must state that the growth principles within the pages have universal application. During my work with diverse nationalities and backgrounds, I have collected stories from people across several creeds, colors, and countries to establish my conclusions and create the ideas I recommend in the book. If applied with intentional consistency and discipline, this will be more than just another book for your library shelf.

This book will become your life companion.

CHAPTER 1

Character:
The Bedrock of Transformation

"Character is like a tree, and reputation is like a shadow.
The shadow is what we think of it; the tree is the real thing."
—Abraham Lincoln

The Google hiring process is quite remarkable. When people think about getting hired at the company, they often imagine a process filled with coding challenges, technical assessments, and brain-teasing interviews. However, what truly sets Google apart is its focus on character. While technical skills matter, Google is just as interested in who you are as a person. Integrity, humility, and teamwork are essential qualities that define a successful candidate. Character is a big deal at Google. The company handles vast amounts of information and trusts its employees to make ethical decisions. It looks for people who are honest, accountable, and committed to doing the right thing, even when no one is watching. Candidates who demonstrate strong moral character stand out because Google knows that trust is the foundation of a great workplace.

Cultural fit is another trait that Google values highly. The company thrives on innovation, and that means being open to new ideas, feedback, and collaboration. It doesn't look for people who think they know it all—it wants individuals who are eager to learn, grow, and contribute to a team. Intellectual arrogance has no place in a culture built on shared knowledge and creativity. Teamwork is at the heart of everything Google does. The company isn't just hiring individuals; it's building dynamic, collaborative teams. The best candidates are those who can work well with others, respect different perspectives, and bring out the best in their colleagues. Google believes that when people work together, they create something far greater than what any one person could achieve alone.

This philosophy is reflected in Google's interview process, where cultural fit is just as important as technical ability. Behavioral questions and real-world problem-solving scenarios help assess how candidates think, communicate, and align with the company's values. The company leadership knows that skills can be taught, but character is what drives long-term success. By prioritizing character over credentials, Google has built a workplace grounded in trust, creativity, and excellence. The focus is on hiring the right people, not just the smartest—an approach that has made Google one of the most sought-after employers in the world.

So, What Is Character?

It took me about five years of in-depth study into the concept before I could gain mastery of the different dimensions of true character. There are six expressions of character, and I will explain each of them:

1. Courage: Facing The Storm

Regardless of your creed or roots in life, one thing is certain: you will face some storms in your lifetime. For some, their storm is similar to a strong wind that blows through their life for a few days or weeks, but for most, the storm they face is a terrible whirlwind, a tornado, that threatens to uproot everything they have ever held dear. Yet, the approach to all storms, whether small or mighty, is precisely the same: You Must Find Courage! Of course, it is easier said than done. The nature of courage is not a vague theoretical idea; it is an action, a response, and a lifestyle that is expressed in the following ways:

Embracing Discomfort: The Growth Zone: Courage is found and practised by taking on new tasks and stepping into unfamiliar territories. While it is far easier to stick to tradition and carry on with what you have always known, there is absolutely no growth to be had when replicating the same old things. Even nature teaches us that adapting to difficult situations is a sure way to become better all-around. The butterfly is one of the most beautiful creatures in the forest, but you cannot fathom just how much change it undergoes by transforming from a hairy black caterpillar to a gorgeous insect with colorful wings and a light frame that we all love. Have you ever paused to ask if it was an easy feat for the butterfly? Do you think it was comfortable for it to leave the protection of the sturdy chrysalis and become so vulnerable and lightweight? It takes courage to leave the easy life behind in a bid to improve, but no improvement comes easily; you just have to face the challenges with courage.

The Ripple Effect of Bold Decisions: On a rainy night in the camp of some Boy Scouts, there arose a series of loud thunderbolts and sharp lightning strikes that terrified even the bravest of the boys. While they all sat up in their tents, holding on tightly to their blankets and wishing the storm would stop, they saw their bicycles outside being pelted with the heavy raindrops. However, none of the boys dared step out of the tent to get the bikes out of the rain and into the cover of the tent. None, save one scrawny little boy, Tom. While the senior scouts looked on, afraid and hesitant, Tom ran into the rain and brought his bike into his tent. He did not stop there. He went back again and again, pushing, dragging, and pulling bike after bike until all twelve bikes were safely inside the tents. It was the highest level of bravery that the scout leader had ever seen throughout his thirty years of organizing camp meetings for the Boy Scouts Organization. Of course, as one would expect, Tom was made captain the next morning, and he was awarded seven merit badges for the bold decision he'd taken. But this isn't the end of the story - decisions made out of courage always generate positive ripple effects. Because of that singular act of boldness, all the boys in the camp that night never lost their respect for Tom. A few decades later, when Tom was considered for the highest political position in that city, each of those boys, along with their scout leader, had glowing words of recommendation for the boy who had not only been but also unselfish enough to help everyone out at a scary time. Tom grew in character through this experience, too. Courageous decisions are hardly ever isolated - they have a way of boosting our psychological strength and reinforcing the confidence we have in ourselves.

Courage in Leadership: Inspiring by Example: Leaders aren't expected to chicken out when things get tough. By the simple meaning of the word, a leader is expected to be at the forefront, driving change. To be at the forefront would mean that you would be the first person to meet the enemy, overcome the obstacles, and chart a new path forward - all these actions take courage. Rather than screaming at the top of their lungs in a bid to belt out a rallying cry, a real leader takes the first step and inspires others to follow. This is exactly why leadership and courage are inseparable. Whether as a company CEO or the captain of a basketball team, courage is required to inspire a team to great success.

Cultivating Everyday Bravery: It takes bravery to lead by example, it takes bravery to make bold decisions, and it certainly takes bravery to embrace discomfort and grow. This is where habit comes in; bravery is not something that happens by sheer coincidence. Rather, it is cultivated by daily silencing the voice of fear in our minds and doing what everyone else is afraid to do. In little things like having enough confidence to express yourself to a person you like, or weightier matters like speaking the truth against a powerful government, bravery must be practiced as a lifestyle. This is true courage.

2. Compassion: The Heart of Leadership

In today's world, with all the craze for wealth and frenzy for fame, it seems as if values like compassion are taking a backseat, or even being forgotten altogether. However, it wasn't always this way, and I would say with full assurance that those who are wealthiest in the way of the world always place a premium on human kindness. A quick study of the presidents and leaders of the organizations and governments indicates that the top ten greatest humans that ever lived were all leaders who embodied compassion. Abraham Lincoln showed real affection to people, friends, and foes alike. Mahatma Gandhi sought peace at every turn because he was a man who cherished human lives. Nelson Mandela never relented in the fight for his people for the singular reason that his heart was strengthened by sheer love for his countrymen and racial equality. At the very heart of leadership, there is always the spirit of empathy.

But first, do I love myself?

Self-Compassion: Your Inner Compass: Psychologically, we project our emotions, feelings, and reasons onto our immediate environment. What this means is that if I have no compassion for myself, I won't be able to express the same for those I lead. First, I have to practise self-love by taking care of my mind, spirit, and body, before taking care of others. I know of a boss who hated going home and, therefore, sometimes kept everyone else in the office past midnight. This man had a disregard for his health, too, and despite being diagnosed with a heart issue, he never took the time to take care of himself.

By the end of his third year as the boss, his branch had the highest percentage of staff resignations. People who worked under him kept leaving the organization until the company could not take it anymore. The man was let go of his role, and the company's fortune improved under the new leader despite the employees never being forced to work overtime. That same year, the former boss died of heart complications, and the company sent some flowers, and that was it.

I learned a great lesson from that experience. Though it may be hard to accept, the truth is that I am the only one responsible for my well-being. And if I don't love and take care of myself, I suffer, and everyone around me suffers too. How can I take care of others if I don't take care of myself first?

Empathy in Action: Building Stronger Teams: How often do we put ourselves in other people's shoes? Do we show compassion by understanding our team members' peculiar challenges and offering support? Do I bother to find out *why* that employee keeps arriving late to work every Wednesday? Or am I the kind of leader who doesn't care about my team members' personal circumstances and state of mind so long as they beat the deadlines and turn in their reports?

Empathy is not just a fancy word to throw around during team meetings and yearly reviews; rather, it is demonstrated in little ways like asking, "How was your weekend?" and genuinely *listening* to the response. Empathy can be as simple as giving a new employee a second chance to complete a task, showing them their mistakes, and putting an arm around their shoulder to encourage them. It's also shown in other ways, like giving bonuses, offering a ride, or taking the team out for dinner after a particularly strenuous day at work. Every available index has proven that **understanding, competent leaders get more productivity out of their team than aggressive, result-driven leaders.**

The Compassionate Leader's Toolkit: I have mentioned a few practical ways to show compassion, but there are many more. This list, a product of decades of experience and research, contains seven simple rules and habits that illustrate leading with compassion.

1. Listen more, speak gently
2. Commend publicly, correct privately
3. Ask for explanations and admit faults
4. Delegate with patience, teach without sarcasm
5. Give incentives, recognize extra efforts
6. Be visible, be accessible, get involved
7. Protect the team, remove slackers

Balancing Compassion with Accountability: The last rule in the toolkit needs extra emphasis. Being compassionate as a leader should never translate to promoting complacency and incompetence. It is truly unfair to the group when some team members keep putting in the hard work while others are loafing around, while the leader keeps treating everyone nicely. This is not what compassion is about. A leader's compassion must always be in the interests of the general group, not for a few sacred cows. And when individuals who, after being taught with patience and given a few second chances, do not take correction, such people must be held accountable. Compassion is kind, but it is also fair.

3. Consistency: The Silent Power

When twin brothers were asked to participate in a three-kilometre exhibition marathon race across their hometown, everyone who heard the announcement was amused by the idea of the competition. The two guys were similar, but non-identical. They were each given twelve days to prepare themselves for the race. The first brother had been involved in several sports activities in high school, and the second leaned more towards academics. So, for those who placed bets on the marathon, it was an easy choice to back the first. The bookmakers promised a rewarding odds of five-to-one for those who backed him to win. Once he saw the odds were fixed, the second brother started practicing the next morning. He started with a hundred meters, and the next day, he pushed himself to cover two hundred more. Each day, this academically inclined twin consistently added an extra two hundred meters to his previous day's run. By the end of the tenth day, just two days before the competition, on his early morning run to cover his first three kilometers, the second-born happened upon his brother.

"Why do you bother?" the athletic firstborn asked. "You know you can't beat me. I am starting my training today," he boasted and winked. "But the next two days are all I need to win."

Rather than explain to his brother that he had been slowly building stamina and speed, the second twin simply smiled and continued his practice.

Well, the day of the exhibition marathon finally arrived, and both runners stood on the starting mark. As everyone in the town lined up on both sides of the road, those who had placed their bets on the firstborn twin started hailing their man. The few people in the crowd who'd taken the risk of backing the second-born clenched their teeth, too agitated to speak.

The gun went off, and the marathon began. The firstborn, an accomplished sprinter and sportsperson in his own right, dashed forward and led the race from the first minute. However, his brother was not perturbed as he steadily gathered his strength and kept his speed fairly uniform – he was not too fast, but he didn't run slowly either. By the middle of the first kilometer, the firstborn was far ahead that he couldn't see his brother on the curvy road. Confident that he was leading with a wide gap, the firstborn started to slow down. The sun was out, his knees started to ache, and his lungs burned. As his backers screamed his name, excited that they had put their money on the right person, the firstborn continued slowing down by the minute, waving to the people as he passed.

By the one-kilometer mark, the firstborn could barely jog. His feet grew heavy, and he suddenly felt a strong desire to have a cold drink. But he knew that was not going to help him, so he went on staggering forward. His brother was still far behind and out of his sight.

The second twin didn't reduce his speed, and he did not increase it. He maintained the same speed he'd started with, and his steady running for the past eleven days profited him. By the end of the second kilometer, the second brother could see his brother right around the next bend, and the screams of the audience on the sides of the road were now at their highest pitch. But the second brother wasn't moved by the cheers. He kept running steadily until he caught up with his brother. And as he passed him and left him behind, he looked at his first brother's face and gave him a big smile. He winked at his twin, said nothing, and kept running.

By the time the second brother could see the finish line right ahead, he looked back and saw his brother staggering along the road, almost fainting. As the winner crossed the line, the first twin finally collapsed on the road, barely able to breathe. The few people who had placed their bets on the second twin ran madly across the road to hug him tightly while the medics rushed towards his brother.

The twins hugged at the end of the marathon, but the lesson was impossible to ignore.

This story remains one of the best ways I have to motivate people: steady little improvements every day will take you farther than a sudden burst of high achievement that cannot be sustained. This principle is further illustrated in four perspectives.

Small Actions, Big Impact: The Compound Effect: Rather than focusing on the biggest, toughest part of the plan or dream, the best strategy is to start with the simplest action or decision required. It is like the popular Navy SEAL habit of always making the bed every single morning. The simplest of actions creates a ripple effect that builds up steadily, and this is the way the greatest achievements are attained. Do several things in a small way, but stay consistent with the input to make a big impact. The multiple simple actions build up into a great effect - whether I am running in a marathon, trying to shed some excess weight, getting to grips with public speaking, or trying to save the planet - the goal must always be to **effect great change through small, consistent steps.**

Building Trust Through Reliability: Consistency is not limited to goal setting. It is also the best way to build character. When I am consistent with the way I approach and respond to things, it builds trust in the people who are around me. Sports come to mind when we talk about trust, reliability, and consistency. Be the gold medal match of an Olympic basketball tournament, or a football World Cup final, if a player is with the ball, the clock is ticking to the last seconds, and two teammates are open to receive a pass and shoot for the goal, in the end, it will all come down to trust and consistency. During practice, who has been more accurate with their shot? This is the question that will be answered a second before making the final pass. Am I consistent enough to be given a once-in-a-lifetime opportunity? If I am, then it becomes easy to trust me. It's that simple.

Consistency in Branding and Communication: In this modern age of digital technology, everyone is a brand in one form or the other. Whether I am running a business or I am a part of an organization, my lifestyle and appearance are all part of my brand. Since my brand determines whether people will be willing to work with me, I must take steps intentionally. Business owners or handlers of social media pages of organizations are taught to stick to the same tone of messaging and generate a unique voice in their ads. Whether as an individual or corporation, the message is the same: keep the brand colors consistent, keep the language consistent, and keep the core values consistent. This is the best way to become memorable even when your name is not mentioned. This is the art of branding and communication.

Overcoming the Plateaus: Staying Consistent When It's Hard: This is a challenging issue for even the world's top coaches. Take basketball, for instance—should a coach treat Michael Jordan the same as every other player? Should one standard apply to the entire team, or should exceptions be made for star contributors? While it can feel difficult—sometimes even impossible—my research into interviews with some of the most successful managers reveals a common thread: in the end, the best leaders apply the same standards of reward and discipline to everyone, regardless of status. When it's tough to maintain that sense of fairness, I remind myself that my actions set the tone for the entire group. And when I'm tempted to compromise my values for short-term gain, I think about the future I'm trying to protect. It's far better to stick with the principles that consistently work than to abandon them for fleeting advantages.

4. Conscience: Your Moral Anchor

What is character without conscience? What is anything really without some conscience? Why do we do the things we do if not for conscience's sake? When the leaders of two world powers have a nuclear weapon at their disposal, is it not conscience that stops one from bringing destruction to humanity while the other decides it was a necessity to detonate it against their enemies? Yet, when millions of lives are negatively impacted by the action, the world focuses on the decision makers and the consequences of the action rather than looking deeper to try to understand the moral background. Conscience drives the very nature of a human being, and it is the source of all our expressions, both good and bad. If you have not paid attention to any of the values so far, please pay attention to this one. The world cannot afford to keep blurring the lines between morality, liberality, and responsibility. It is sad to see just how low humans have now gone in the way we act towards others, how we respond to other people's pain, and the lengths we are willing to go to in gaining fame and fortune. Dear reader, this is my earnest plea in this moment: please, listen to the voice of your conscience and always do what is right.

Ethical Decision-Making in Turbulent Times: It can be quite daunting to stick to the voice of conscience when things are not all good and dandy, yet it is in these kinds of moments that one's character is purified and reinforced. The strength of a crucible is only proven when the fire burns hot, and its marble never gives way. A protest that began as a peaceful march against police brutality in my city soon turned to an all-out war, and in the aftermath, blame was traded all around. A panel was set up, and a man was called as the principal witness to give a true account of things. Now, this man had a name for honesty and integrity, so both sides of the case trusted him to speak the truth. However, things are not always so black-and-white, and our man knew this well. During the protests, he had seen how protesters had picked up arms against the police, and he knew that the people were not innocent. Yet, it was a struggle because the city was calling for the Chief of Police's head. The man of truth knew that his words would sway the course of judgment. His wife begged him to recuse himself and step away from the case. His children insisted that he must back his people. Our man of truth was caught in a dangerous dilemma. However, he knew the right thing to do from the beginning. His conscience could never allow him to keep silent, or worse, tell a lie. This man followed his conscience. He spoke with much compassion about the public's role in the violence and pleaded with the government to lay the matter to rest. As his conscience led him, he didn't just share his story; he went as far as settling the matter and making recommendations on the steps forward. This is what I have imbibed in my life, and this is what I coach others. **Do the right thing, uphold ethical standards, and follow your conscience.**

Aligning Actions with Values: A Framework: Several companies and leaders list out strong core values without ever imbuing the values into their culture or lifestyle. This is not the way to build conscience. It's one thing to talk about integrity; do

I practice what I preach? The A-to-E framework below can help us translate our values into real actions.

a. Add up all the core values and arrange them in order of strength.
b. Build step-by-step definitions that illustrate these values in real-life scenarios.
c. Create cases where the values can be tested and highlight the obstacles to execution.
d. Determine the first response, and have a Plan B response for every case study.
e. Engage people in how to demonstrate these values to assist them.

Building an Ethical Organization from the Ground Up: The best time to execute an organization's value strategy is when the organization is still manageable in size, and everything comes through the leader. This is the time when we can dictate the ethical structure and culture we want the organization to stand for. As we recruit people to join the vision, we must ensure that their values align with our organization's. I have also learned that one has to quickly call people to order when they begin to veer off course in a bid to meet the organization's goals. If you want an organization to prioritize openness, the offices in the workplace may be designed so that all the walls are made of glass; these are practical ways to build ethics into the organization right from the beginning.

When Values Clash: Navigating Moral Dilemmas: What if I find myself in a hard place where upholding one value would mean that I have to let go of another? For example, you value friendship and loyalty, and you also see yourself as a person of integrity. However, your friend has damaged some company property and then patched it up and returned it to its place without making a report. No one knew about this, and he only told you in confidence because of your friendship. Would you stay loyal to your friend or stand for integrity? Life is not always simple, and the answers are not often straightforward. What if you are in a working relationship where your partners or leaders have opposing values, or they don't place much emphasis on the values you hold dear? What do you do then? The dilemma is quite complex, so my recommendation will be simple: Look at the bigger picture and take a fair stand, not just to yourself, but to everyone involved. This is a rule I employ when I am caught in a difficult place. In the case of the example I gave, looking at the bigger picture may mean you buy the damaged item and replace it, and then ask your friend to let the company know that the property was damaged but has been replaced. Looking at the bigger picture has pulled me out of several fixes, and it always helps when you take a look at the solution, not the problem.

5. Courtesy: The Fine Art of Respect

I don't know if you are familiar with the story of the young doorman who became a director. Every morning, right at the crack of dawn, he would be in front of the great skyscraper that housed the National Bank, and every morning, with a smile that made his eyes shine, this man would greet all the employees and clients that came in through the door. If it happened to be raining, he would step into the rain and offer an umbrella as a person stepped out of the car, and if someone happened to be stuck indoors, this man would call a cab from the street and convince the driver to come as close to the building as possible. If a person thanked him for his assistance, he would burst into laughter and say, "Thank *you*, kind sir/madam, for thanking me!" It was not just the words he used, but the way he said them. With his characteristic grin and cheerfulness, as if each day was the best day of his life, he never forgot to show courtesy.

This went on for several years, and this young man never changed. He treated the daughter of the company cook the same way he treated the CEO's wife. He always had a kind word to say, regardless of the circumstances. After this man had been a doorman for four years, the company underwent a digital restructuring that meant non-essential workers had to be replaced. Naturally, the company started from the bottom. The decision was that they would put a revolving electronic door in the building's entrance and let all their doormen go.

Once the decision had been made, our young doorman received his letter of dismissal along with a severance package, and he began to pack the few things he had in his locker in the basement of the building. It was while he was cleaning out his locker that some of the staff came rushing into the basement. They had just heard of the decision, and they had come to wish the good man a final goodbye. Of course, as was his custom, the young doorman bowed as he shook hands, he laughed, and comforted those who were sad for him. He made jokes about his situation and told the crowd that he would come back as a machine in his next life. The people laughed, and the young man made his way out of the basement.

However, he found that the door had been blocked by a large man in a blue suit. When the young man looked closely, he quickly bowed and cheerfully greeted the man at the door. It was the company CEO, and the entire staff, all standing behind the doorman, who looked on with smiles. They knew what was coming; they were in on the plan.

"You have been so good to everyone in this room," the CEO told the young man. Then he turned to the employees and asked loudly. "Who wants this good man to join their team?" All the hands in the room went straight up. The young doorman was on the verge of tears. In the end, it was agreed that the young man would join the Human Resources department because of his congeniality. He was given an office right at the window overlooking the entrance door he had manned for years. In another two years, our young man had acquired enough education to be assigned a new role as a deputy director. When the director moved to another company, it was a unanimous decision to make the young man the director of the department.

Humans have made such great advancements in science, art, and commerce, but nothing has ever been able to replace the power of genuine courtesy. In today's world, because of its rarity, courtesy now gains greater rewards. I will illustrate this point from four perspectives.

First Impressions That Last: The Science of Likeability: Several studies have proven that people don't need more than ten seconds after meeting someone before deciding whether they want to meet this person again or not. I think I can understand this. There are over seven billion people in the world, and each of us meets less than ten percent of this number throughout our entire lifetime. Now, even if we live for a hundred years, there is a very high probability that we will not meet most people more than once. Unless we are restricted to a space with the same human beings for most of our lives, we will not get a chance to meet a large percentage of people more than the first time. This is pure mathematics, and it is the basis of the science of likability. Because our subconscious mind knows that most people will get a single chance at impressing us, most of our senses are heightened when we meet someone new. We listen more, pay more attention to them, and get our guards up quickly. This is both a psychological defence and a desire to maximize our lifetime. No one wants to waste their time on meeting people who offer no value whatsoever, and this is why we often tune out after the first ten seconds of interaction. Our mind looks forward to the next person, rather than the next meeting. Understanding this science has helped me over the years. When I meet people for the first time, I am determined to leave a memorable mark on their minds, and I do this either by the firmness of my handshake, asking a question about their name, making a joke, complimenting their look, or commenting on what they did. This is all a strategy for me to stay at the top of their mind so they'll remember me at subsequent meetings.

Navigating Cultural Sensitivities in a Global World: The world is a global village now, and we meet people from many different backgrounds. So, we need to be quite adaptable in the way we show courtesy to people. Some simple research beforehand will help greatly, and then ask questions. If I am unsure of the prevailing cultural rules of a new environment, it is best not to take a chance and risk offending people whom I have just met. Remember what I said about first impressions? In such situations, watch how more experienced people show their courtesy, pay attention to the little details, and be sure things are acceptable before acting. If you somehow make an error in judgment, apologize quickly and rectify the action. Globally, I have found that people are more forgiving of strangers who attempt to embrace their culture, but it is much more impressive to get it right on the first attempt! Again, we learn by doing our research, asking questions, and paying attention.

Digital Courtesy: Etiquette for the Modern Age: The digital footprints we leave behind through emails, social media comments, photos, and videos **are never going to disappear.** People have lost opportunities of a lifetime because of an old post they made a decade ago. The importance of digital etiquette, therefore, can never be overstated. The two rules I coach people on are: 1. You do not have to post anything online. 2. Read your comments back to yourself before sending them. Once we send out a post on the internet, our footprint remains permanently in cyberspace. We may come back to delete it with regret or an apology, but our words remain in the cloud. This is why we must be intentionally courteous and respectful when online, even more so to people we don't know personally. I have realized that it is best to show class when provoked and keep my thoughts to myself when the world is screaming about a trending, yet sensitive issue. This way, I protect my name and my person.

The ROI of Respect: How Courtesy Impacts the Bottom Line: The gains of respect and courtesy are diverse. From being recommended for greater opportunities, like the young doorman was, to preserving a reputation carefully built through hard work, there are real-life advantages attached to courtesy. Remember this: we have nothing to lose by showing class and courtesy, but we have everything to gain by being respectful. Let me repeat that more simply: there is no single disadvantage of being respectful, while one can lose *everything* just because of some perceived act of disrespect.

6. Commitment: The Fuel for Success

"Those who want quick successes will meet with lasting failure." I heard this quote once, and at first, it seemed rather dark and exaggerated. It took several hours of deep thought before I could embrace its truth. My life has taught me that there is no point starting a journey if I am not committed to sticking with it to the end. Often, what separates the greatest decision makers from those who fail is simply commitment. More than half of business start-ups fail within the first two years for this same reason: lack of commitment. It is this value that has been lost in our generation today, and has now resulted in divorce rates being at an all-time high. **Commitment has a direct implication on our chances of being successful at anything in life**, yet, sadly, it is a character trait that is becoming increasingly scarce. Let us examine how commitment translates to success.

From Vision to Reality: The Power of Unwavering Focus: Twenty university graduates sat in a room, and each one was asked the same question: "Where do you see yourself in the next ten years?" As each of them started talking about their plan, mostly memorized and well-rehearsed, it soon became clear to the panel that there were only two ladies amongst the twenty who had any real chance of going on to achieve great things. The two young women spoke with clarity and focus, each centered on a single idea, while the other eighteen shared a mix of plans and dreams. Unlike their peers, those two graduates had a clear, singular objective. It was no surprise when, a few years later, one of them launched her own tech servicing company—just as she had described to the panel. Focus is a reflection of commitment.

Just as we can't devote ourselves to ten romantic partners, we can't commit to ten life goals. Everyone has a vision, but turning that vision into reality requires choosing a path and staying with it until the goal is achieved. That's what true commitment looks like.

Overcoming Obstacles with Determination: Singleness of purpose also helps us remain undaunted in the face of overwhelming challenges. The university graduate lady who opened that tech company had to struggle with bankruptcy three years into the business, but she pulled through it simply because she knew that it was either success or absolute defeat. There was no fallback plan for her, and that made the difference on several occasions when she became threatened by the challenges that face every new business. Obstacles will arise, but is your resolution strong enough to keep going? This is why commitment is a rewarding character trait - it compels us to work on solutions rather than giving up.

The Psychology of Commitment: Why We Stick (or Don't): There's a science behind positive stubbornness. It's the same force that makes us determined to finish what we've started. It's also why there are so few college dropouts in countries with struggling economies and limited opportunities. Who wants to give up the one path that feels like a guaranteed shot at success? Who would walk away from an education when they know how much suffering and sacrifice went into getting them there? We stick with our decisions because of two things: the sacrifices we've already made and the rewards we believe are waiting for us. Once we've paid such a high price, it's hard to call it quits, and that can work against us. Sometimes we keep going even when something no longer serves us, simply because we've come too far to turn back. That's called the *sunk cost fallacy*, and it's a trap many people fall into without realizing it. That's why the second part matters. We hold on because of the benefits we think are still ahead. This is the psychology behind commitment, with sacrifice and reward working together to keep us moving forward.

Building a Culture of Commitment in Your Organization: Now that we have all agreed that commitment is a great characteristic, how do we convince others in an organization to stay committed to our goals?

1. Explain why things are done the way they are.
2. Track results and monitor individual outputs.
3. Invest in people and convince them to learn.
4. Reward extra effort and improve discipline.
5. Create a clear path for growth in the organization.
6. Be more than a boss; be an ally.
7. Build a small team of core members.

As I wrap up this chapter on CHARACTER, it is only fitting that I explain that there will be bad days in this journey. I have had such days aplenty; everyone has. However, keeping our eye on the destination should help us stay on track no matter what happens along the way. When courage backfires, compassion is taken for granted, consistency sways and breaks, conscience becomes conflicted, and we see no reason to be courteous, we must remember to stay committed to the cause we have started - keep building true character! There is a reward for all this, and more than that, this is the only true way to live a full life!

CHAPTER 2

Creativity:
Igniting the Spark

"Creativity is seeing what others see and thinking what no one else ever thought." —Albert Einstein

---

When Salman Khan started tutoring his cousins online, he had no idea he was laying the foundation for a global educational revolution. What began as simple video lessons to help family members eventually transformed into Khan Academy—a platform that has reshaped how people learn. Khan's creativity in using technology to make education accessible has turned a small idea into a worldwide movement. However, this all started with a problem: traditional education was expensive, rigid, and inaccessible to many. Instead of accepting these limitations like many before him had done, Khan found a way to break them. By using short, engaging videos, he made complex subjects easier to understand. He reimagined the classroom experience. With interactive exercises and a self-paced learning model, Khan Academy has given millions of students a chance to learn anytime, anywhere, and at their own speed.

This academy's impact has been extraordinary. Students who once struggled now have free access to high-quality lessons, teachers have the means to supplement their instruction, and entire communities have benefited from an education system that no longer depends on wealth or location. What started as one man's creative solution has become a driving force in educational access around the world. Khan's success proves that creativity is not just about art or innovation—it's also about seeing challenges as opportunities. His story reminds us that with imagination and determination, we can transform the world in ways we never thought possible.

There are probably a thousand and one ways to solve every single problem known to man; however, over ninety percent of people will only consider the one solution without giving any attention to the other one thousand. This is the way the world has always been, and sadly, it seems that we will continue like this in the future. I have been in long strategic meetings where we spent five to six hours debating about solution A, considering its pros and cons, and fiercely arguing for its merits and demerits, without ever entertaining possibilities B, C, and so on. What I have realized is that, in teams and places where creativity is not encouraged, stagnancy and decline aren't far away. Creativity is simply the ability to create, to bring something into existence, and to establish a new set of principles that were previously unknown.

Every creative process starts with the ability to imagine. Imagination is the bedrock of creativity, and we must keep encouraging people to use their imagination. Picasso captured this matter quite accurately when he explained that everyone was born as an artist of some sort, but the real problem is remaining a creative artist as we grow up. With how kids are being shouted down, shut up, and silenced, I fear for the next generation. When a kid says or does something out of the ordinary, their creative nature must be nurtured and supported rather than being ridiculed and punished. Classroom teachers and parents have a great impact on the creativity of the human race - they are the first line of people who will fan the flames of creativity and encourage young people's curiosity.

1. Curiosity: The Wellspring of Innovation

A TV advert made waves in my home country some decades ago. In it, a small girl walked through a supermarket with her mom and asked questions as they moved from the bakery aisle to the meat section. The mother's smile as she answered each question warmed the TV audience's heart, and the ad became a countrywide sensation. I still remember the last question that the beautiful girl asked in the last scene. "Why is water wet?" Her mom laughed kindly at this question, and those of us who loved the advert did too, but I found the lesson in the seemingly "childish" questions quite poignant.

When the ad aired, I had already spent two decades in the world, yet I'd never thought to ask why water is wet. It struck me that the little girl in the ad would probably soon understand water molecules better than I ever had. That realization made me start asking the question myself, and in the process of searching for an answer, I discovered things I'd never known before.

This experience reinforced why curiosity should be encouraged, not just in schools, but also in workplaces, organizations, and life in general. Asking "why?" leads to a deeper understanding than simply assuming you know. It's from that deeper understanding that true innovation often emerges.

However, not all curiosity leads to innovation. So, what makes curiosity innovative? What are the elements that turn a question into a breakthrough?

Asking the Right Questions: The Art of Inquiry: The first step to creative curiosity is knowing what sort of question to ask. Questions must be designed in a way that provokes the mind to seek solutions. First, you must define the question's purpose. Before asking a question, we must first ask ourselves, "What do I want to learn or achieve?" Some questions are asked just to ridicule the other party - avoid such lines of inquiry. Also, avoid questions that force people to respond in anger. There is no need to be offensive. We must be specific with the question we ask; this will help us frame the question correctly. For example, a pupil raises a hand in class and asks the mathematics teacher, "What is the final answer to this word problem?" This question, though clear and relevant, will not solve the student's real problem nor help him understand what is being taught. However, the question can be framed differently: "Please, Sir, how do I find the answer to this word problem?" This manner of question will not only please the teacher, but it will also help the student to understand the process. As a rule, asking *why* and *how* gives more clarity and understanding than asking *when* or *who*. While the latter goes directly to the conclusion, the former helps to think creatively through the process.

a. Other tips to constructively frame a question include:
b. Ask for explanations with follow-up questions: *yes* and *no* answers require follow-ups.
c. Ask open-ended questions: replace "Did you like the plan?" with "What do you think about the plan?"

d. Ask with a genuine interest in understanding their mindset and avoid assumptions.
e. Show respect for their perspective, even if you disagree.
f. Allow the other person to answer in detail without interrupting.

Embracing the Unknown: Comfort with Ambiguity: Anyone who has ever walked into a philosophy class—aside from the frustration of hard-to-pronounce names and the constant disagreements among early thinkers—quickly learns to accept confusion as a natural part of the process. Philosophies are not discussed under the assumption of right or wrong. No, they are just perspectives that are different, yet true. And we will have to realize that what is true is not the same as what is correct. I know this sounds paradoxical, but it is a necessity for gaining creative curiosity. Every question will not possess a straight answer, and that is alright. Embracing this reality of ambiguity helps us stay open-minded and creative in our solution process.

Curiosity Quotient: Measuring and Enhancing Your CQ: Finding out my level of curiosity will help me improve on ways to ask more relevant questions and seek answers. This is what the CQ helps with. The CQ index helps us evaluate our present instinctive inclination to seek understanding, investigate methods, explore fresh perspectives, and embrace the unknown. Although the EQ (emotional quotient) and IQ (intelligence quotient) are more popular measurements, the CQ is just as crucial in determining creativity levels in leaders. Simple steps to measure CQ include:

1. Assessing our openness to new experiences, tolerance for uncertainty, and question-asking habit.

2. Developing a curiosity assessment tool that determines reading habits, social curiosity behavior, and problem-solving techniques.
3. Analyzing scenario-based challenges, like the time taken to learn a new skill before giving up. How often does one step out of comfort zone to attempt unfamiliar tasks?
4. Asking for feedback from friends, colleagues, and supervisors about one's curiosity level.
5. Scoring and classifying the results of the self-assessment and behavioral analysis into High CQ (thrives in new environments, active curiosity), Moderate CQ (needs extra motivation to embrace new challenges), and Low CQ (avoids unfamiliar processes, sticks to routine).

Creating a Culture of Curiosity in Teams & Organizations: As a leader in my team, I take on the responsibility of building a culture of creativity through curiosity. This involves more than sitting at the head of the table in a conference and encouraging people to ask questions at the end of a presentation! In teams and organizations, building a culture of inquiry involves *asking* questions, even the most obvious ones. As leaders, we must also learn to delegate difficult tasks that will provoke our team members' minds and encourage them to get out of their comfort zones. I do this sometimes by posing extremely difficult case studies and offering a reward to the team members who solve the problem. This has a way of generating a high level of curiosity amongst the team. I also recommend designing the walls of our workplaces with frames containing philosophical questions that exercise the mind. Most importantly, I try to applaud questions asked publicly and reward the best answers. Whether the team is out celebrating a contract over drinks or gathered in the office coming up with strategies, the team leaders must ask questions, be they personal or complex.

2. Create: Turning Ideas into Reality

The creative process starts with curiosity, but it does not stop there. The inquisitive mind asks questions, but the value of these questions and their answers lies only in their deployment to solve actual problems. If I had a partner with a low CQ, the first thing I would do is to break their routine and force their mind to seek answers. However, this is only an initial step. After getting curious, one must start to create. I love to sit in and listen to ideas flying around during my team's brainstorming strategy/ideation sessions because of the intelligence on full display. Intelligent ideas are not enough, however. I have always argued that the execution techniques are more important than the ideation process. The world, I have found, is full of people who know what to do, while the number of people who actually do (act or execute) is always minimal. How do we turn ideas into reality? This is a question that has been asked for centuries.

From Concept to Prototype: A Step-by-Step Guide: Regardless of the kind of solution, product, or service, once the team has settled on the best idea for execution, what follows is the critical stage of transforming this concept into a methodical structure that sees your concept grow from an idea to a fully-functioning process. Whether your organization is seeking to launch a new product or you are planning to build a new home for your family, the developmental stages involved in all ideas generally follow the same flow as mapped below:

1. Clearly state the problem you are solving or the need you are fulfilling.
2. Articulate your aim & objectives, mission & vision, purpose & goals.
3. List all the essential product features and intended users or target audience.
4. Study similar products or competing services and identify your edge or improvement points.
5. Conduct research into the market and product through surveys, interviews, and questionnaires.
6. Sketch to visualize your idea through drawings, flow diagrams, or storyboards.
7. Establish a set of criteria and benchmarks to evaluate success.
8. Source resources, budget, and skilled individuals to execute the idea.
9. Design your prototype, test, and get feedback from experts.
10. Launch an improved prototype and prepare for scale-up.

Overcoming Creative Blocks: Techniques for Unleashing Ideas: Even the most creative people - be they writers, artists, or engineers - have to grapple with the problem of mental block where their ideas just seem to cease, and the creative juice just stops flowing. The best creatives, however, know what to do to get through these momentary lapses. I have spoken to several imaginative problem solvers, and their approach to regaining their power can be summed up into three action points: (i) Change your environment, such as going for a walk or changing your work station. (ii) Enjoy a hobby: allowing yourself to relax can reactivate you and help your mind focus. (iii) Design a structure of working: break the project into small, manageable tasks and build a habit of working at a precise time of the day to help you overcome the problem of not knowing how to start.

The Creator's Toolkit: Essential Resources for Making: Certain tools are required for every creative process. These resources, though diverse and non-standard, have helped me find inspiration and improved my productivity over the years. I have met many creative people in my career, and this list also includes those things that they would recommend to anyone seeking inspiration.

a. Notebooks, diaries, and sticky notes
b. Landscape painting & framed quotes
c. Ergonomic chairs, desks, & shelves
d. Stopwatch, clock, & calendar
e. Music, headphones, & speakers
f. Books, magazines, & journals
g. Whiteboard & colored markers
h. Rubik's Cube, puzzles, & chess

While this list is not exhaustive and doesn't include the more essential and personal tools like a computer, the listed resources will help sharpen your mind.

Balancing Creativity and Practicality in Business: I won't pretend there haven't been times in my life when creativity and business goals have not been at loggerheads. This is a recurrent dilemma in many organizations. There is usually a more practical cost-saving technique of doing things, but this method is routine and uninspiring, while on the other hand, we also have the untested, bogus way of achieving the same goal with maximum creativity. The question to a team lead or business manager is, "Which choice do you make?" Of course, my advice is always to gradually introduce some creativity into the proven and trusted traditional way of doing business. A process that has ten steps, for example, can remain practical for eight of the steps, and then be creative with the remaining two. A point to note, however, is that a business that completely shuns creativity will soon die. So will a business that establishes full creativity without retaining the practical aspect. Finding a balance is key.

3. Craft: Honing Your Skills

This story may sound familiar—it's something that has likely happened to someone you know. I once read about a group of boys who attended the same elementary school. Among them was Sam, a gifted cartoonist. He spent countless hours sketching with pencils, creating original stories and characters in a unique and beautiful style. His talent quickly became obvious, and before long, other boys began paying him for complete cartoon story sketches. The more he drew, the better he became.

To everyone in the group, Sam's future seemed clear. While most of the boys were still unsure about what they wanted to do when they grew up, it was obvious Sam was destined to be an artist. He was simply too talented not to be one.

However, reality often takes a different path than expected. Sam stopped drawing in high school and decided to pursue a career in medicine instead. Having set aside his artistic skills, his talent for drawing faded over time.

Sometimes when I think about this story, I feel sympathy for the boy. I wish I'd known him so I could ask some questions. I think I know why he couldn't pick up drawing again. It is a fact that there is no craft without practice. Any skill left undeveloped will not stay at a constant level, but will instead deteriorate until it is no more. Let's examine how honing skills and talent can transform into a craft from four perspectives.

The Journey to Mastery: The 10,000-Hour Rule Revisited: Hugely popularized by journalist Malcolm Gladwell, through his best-selling book, *Outliers: The Story of Success*, the 10,000-Hour Rule states that it takes approximately ten thousand hours of deliberate practice to gain mastery over any skill. Gladwell based the rule on the study done on elite performers, including musicians, athletes, and chess players. The rule is the bedrock of the Chinese *Kung-Fu* schools, where a pupil is expected to go over a single fight maneuver thousands of times until they can execute each technique blindfolded. The hours of consistent practice accumulate, spanning about three hours daily for ten years until 10,000 hours are achieved. Although there have been several suggestions that other factors like innate ability and environment play a role in gaining mastery over a skill, it is incontestable that anyone who seeks to achieve greatness in any endeavour, and convert a craft into profit, must be consistent in developing the craft until it becomes a part of their existence.

Deliberate Practice: Strategies for Rapid Skill Acquisition: Let me quickly point out that consistent practice of a skill is not done arbitrarily. There are strategies to use when you want to learn a new skill - and yes, you can acquire a skill by constant strategic practice. If you follow these simple principles with discipline and intentionality, you can become a master at your chosen craft.

1. The first thing to know is that learning a skill requires patience.
2. Identify the skill and define the craft you want to master; I strongly recommend practising one skill at a time.
3. Plan a structured routine with milestones and indices to measure your mastery level.
4. Simply learning isn't enough; you must structure your practice based on difficulty levels, starting from the easiest.
5. For every step completed, push your limit further in the subsequent practice.
6. Always ask for feedback, correct errors, and then repeat the improved process.
7. Only take on harder challenges once the previous level has been completely mastered.

The Art of Feedback: Using Criticism to Fuel Growth: App creators have mastered this simple hack to ensure constant improvement. On every app store, you will always see the option of rating the app and leaving a comment. Some app developers have even gone as far as offering rewards for customers who provide feedback. The engineers building apps and solving problems have realized that nothing ensures growth and development as much as external criticism. We must all create a channel for feedback in our lives. Of course, it always sounds nicer to our ears when we hear commendations and positive reviews; however, when people correct or criticize us, it is important not to see it as an attack on our person or be outrightly dismissive of such comments. If properly managed and channeled to focus on the message rather than the manner with which it was delivered, we will always grow in leaps and bounds. Other people can spot our flaws more easily than we can, and if we are planning to turn a craft into a business, then we must listen to the people who would require the craft and be willing to pay for our service or commodities.

Craftsmanship in the Digital Age: Blending Tradition and Technology: The major crafts developed by humankind evolved from three basic human needs: food, shelter, and clothing. As a result, the earliest craftsmen were primarily hunters, farmers, fishermen, builders, and tailors. Even before the invention of books, early humans were already using metal tools to enhance their crafts.

Interestingly, there is a clear connection between the strategies used by early humans and the developments of our digital age. Just as traditional crafts drove the advancement of science and engineering through invention and tool improvement, the digital era has progressed in much the same way. A closer look at the history of computing reveals that both financial and human investments have consistently followed practical needs.

For example, Microsoft Excel became a major force in the rise of personal computing because it offered businesspeople a faster way to manage their work. Later, as mobile phones became widely used, industries shifted their focus to mobile apps and software development to meet new demands.

Recognizing that digital crafts are not fundamentally different from traditional ones should remind us to apply the same core business principles. Chief among these is the understanding that any craft—digital or otherwise—that meets a genuine human need will always have value. Ultimately, success comes from blending digital tools with timeless business fundamentals.

4. Cognition: Sharpening Your Mental Edge

Only a handful of things are more important than the mind. You cannot arrive at a point in reality without your mind conceiving the journey; therefore, there can be no creativity without cognition. Cognition involves several mental processes that deal with collecting, processing, storing, and using knowledge to establish understanding. In other words, cognition consists of any activities that help us to perceive through our senses, think things through, learn new ideas and recall old ones during a decision-making process, and make choices. These processes are essential for humans as they're one of the major differences between us and other animals. This ability controls how we interact with our environment and with other humans.

Cognition is mainly biological, with several parts of the brain working in a coordinated manner with specialized functions. The cerebral cortex is the site of all cognitive functions in the human brain, and it is divided into four lobes. The frontal lobe is the seat of intelligence and is involved in voluntary decision-making. The parietal lobe oversees spatial awareness, the temporal lobe deals with memory and stored information, while the occipital lobe controls visual processing. It is a systematic interplay between these lobes that forms what we call the "mind." Some level of understanding of how cognition develops will certainly help us to improve our minds and sharpen our mental functions.

Mind Mapping for Clarity: Organizing Complex Thoughts: The world is currently experiencing an overload of information, and distractions are screaming for our attention. Being able to sit still and think things through has become quite a challenge, and the mind has become generally dulled by entertainment, making it difficult for it to process complex thoughts. Mind mapping, however, is an efficient method that has helped me to visually put my thoughts together, regardless of how complex they may seem. It has also helped me to properly plan, brainstorm, and solve problems. So, what are the tips that I use for mind mapping?

1. Identify the central idea, define the main question you want to solve, and write it down.
2. Draw all the themes, subtopics, and categories that represent the central idea. For example, if the central idea is to solve the problem in a relationship, the categories can include: time management, expression, communication, expectations, etc. These subtopics must be precisely labeled and further expanded if necessary.
3. The use of images, shapes, and visual cues can also help to emphasize connections between subtopics. The same color will represent similar parts of the central idea. For example, expression and communication, in the previous illustration, can be colored the same to show their connection.
4. Collaboration is a big part of mind mapping. Discuss ideas with people and ask questions as they keep breaking down all your sub-themes with further points and relevant examples.
5. When the ideas for solutions arise, organize them against the problem question. This will help you to simplify and summarize major action points from your map.
6. Revise, update, and reorganize your map whenever necessary. Remember to be flexible.

Cognitive Flexibility in a Changing World: How quickly can I adapt my ideas and habits when situations and reality change or new information comes to light? Many creative people have told me the same thing. Flexibility plays a critical role in every creative process, from directing a blockbuster movie to erecting a skyscraper. As you explore your cognitive powers, listen to circumstances and adapt where necessary. Here are some of the strategies I use to strengthen my cognitive flexibility:

- I maintain a growth mindset by asking questions and approaching problems from different angles. I also share my thoughts with experts to get fresh perspectives.

- I never assume. I have found that assumptions and hasty conclusions block the mind from being fully cognitive. When you assume, you stop your brain from working to its full capacity.

- I try to design at least three solutions to each problem, even including unconventional solutions, so that if one approach does not work, switching strategies is easier.

- Now and then, I shake things up in my daily routine, travel to new places, and take up new hobbies outside my interests. This helps me develop flexibility.

- I alternate between completely different tasks, work on memory exercises, and engage in debates that oppose my view.

These habits, alongside the openness to accept uncertainties and ask for feedback, help to keep the cognitive functions quite flexible, enabling us to solve complex problems and thrive with innovation in a drastically changing world.

Enhancing Mental Performance: Nutrition, Exercise, & Sleep: These three components are essential to keep the mind fit and sharp. Why do we not perform well in tests when we lack food or sleep? It is because the brain can not function optimally without these components. Apart from improving mindfulness, exercises promote the growth of neurons in the hippocampus and increase blood flow, particularly to the brain, enabling sharper reaction times. Sleep, on the other hand, is crucial for restoring brain functions and solidifying memories. Our creativity and problem-solving skills get a good boost when we sleep well. Nutrition supplies all the necessary nutrients and energy that the brain cells need to perform their functions efficiently. Glucose keeps the energy levels optimal and provides mental clarity and focus. Vitamins are also needed by neurotransmitters for memory and learning. Tryptophan is a protein found in bananas that enhances mood. These are just a few examples of how food directly impacts our cognitive abilities.

Experts advise we get 150 minutes of simple aerobic exercise every week, get seven hours of good sleep every night, and eat a well-balanced diet. A synergy among these three components helps to establish a great foundation for peak mental performance.

Overcoming Cognitive Biases in Decision Making: Humans generally show biases in cognition by seeking shortcuts through lapses in judgment that result from the brain's lazy attempt to simplify decision making. Have you found yourself looking for reasons to confirm what you initially assumed? That is confirmation bias, and it is a cognitive bias. We overcome this bias by reflecting on past decisions and finding out how our wrong assumptions have caused wrong decisions. We must also slow down when making decisions and spend time to analyze each matter individually, rather than making assumptions without looking deeply into the root. Some questions I ask myself to overcome bias include: "Is this truly the best I can do?", "What are the other alternatives?", "Am I not focusing on the short-term instead of the long-term?" I do my best to be brutally honest with myself when I reflect on these questions, and I have found that this is the only way I can be truly free of cognitive biases. You have to think about what you are thinking about – this is a deeper level of decision-making.

5. Consolidation: Building Your Legacy

What if we lived in a world where no one left anything behind when they were gone? What if every generation left with all their contributions, forcing the next to start from scratch? How can one leave something behind if they don't create anything meaningful that can transcend time? The consolidation of human achievements is crucial for our survival as a species, and the more we create, the more we evolve. Innovations like the computer, mobile phone, digital camera, airplane, and even vaccines didn't exist just a century ago. Yet today, they are some of the most common tools and possessions worldwide. Many of these breakthroughs came from individuals—some as young and educated as you—who developed strategies and conducted research that turned early inventions, no matter how rudimentary, into solutions for long-standing problems.

There have been countless stories of people lying on their deathbeds, asking those around them, "What have I lived for? Ninety years of life, and what do I have to show for it?" It often takes considerable effort from their loved ones to reassure them, and yes, they have families, yet still, they question the meaning of their lives. What I've learned is that many of us want to do something meaningful with our time on earth. We seek to make an impact in some way, and when we fail to achieve that, our hearts feel empty, regardless of the wealth or family we leave behind. A person's legacy must be more than just their bank balance or the number of children they have.

How then do we consolidate a fulfilling legacy?

Identifying Your Unique Contribution to the World: Elon Musk didn't just dream of reaching space—he set out to revolutionize how humanity gets there. When he founded SpaceX, his goal was not limited to building rockets; it was to make space travel accessible and affordable for mankind in the future. However, his road to success was anything but smooth. SpaceX faced failure after failure. Rockets exploded, test flights crashed, and setbacks threatened to shut the company down. Many would have given up. Musk, however, saw each failure as a stepping stone rather than a dead end. He poured his resources, energy, and determination into refining his vision, refusing to let obstacles define the outcome. That persistence paid off in the end. SpaceX accomplished what had once seemed impossible— creating reusable rockets that dramatically reduced the cost of space travel. The company became the first private entity to send a spacecraft to the International Space Station, breaking barriers that had long been controlled by government agencies. What was once science fiction became reality, all because of relentless innovation and an unwillingness to accept limits. Elon Musk's story is not just about space travel—it's also about the power of innovation and purpose. This is a lesson I have lived my life by. Do your best at everything you can do, and you will identify your unique path through life. No one was born with a clear direction of what they should do; we all stumbled upon the talents, skills, and careers that made a difference in our lives and helped us make a difference in the world. I ask five questions that can help everyone identify their unique gifts to the world:

- Identify your strengths: Which talents, work, or skills do you often receive commendation for?
- Reflect on your passion: Apart from what you can do (skills), what excites and fulfils you?
- Find a need to fulfil: In your community or industry, is there a gap that your skill and passion can help fill?
- Embrace challenge and be consistent: Are you willing to hold on to the paths you have chosen when the odds are stacked against you?
- And finally: Are you happy to keep doing this for the rest of your life and pass it on to the next generation?

When one finds an answer to each of these questions, then a path has been found.

From Ideation to Impact: Bringing Big Ideas to Life: Let me go back to Musk's story for a bit. The question is, at what point did the man decide to try building space rockets? How do big ideas form? Where do they come from? How do we bring them to life? Let us look at some history to help us understand the process of ideation to impact.

a. Believe in the plan: Musk had always been fascinated by flight and mechanics, and he had drawn sketches and made scientific calculations about his big idea. However, this was something that had never been successfully done before. So, he needed a lot of belief in his idea. The physics was correct, the mathematics was right, but big ideas need more than theory. If doubts persist, tackle the doubts first by proving the theory before setting out to execute. This is the first step to execution.

b. Conduct repeated experiments: The reality of the world can sometimes disrupt even the best-laid plans, but through consistent testing, you can easily identify mistakes and find areas for improvement.

c. Improve and persevere: Musk ran his businesses to fund his SpaceX dream, and the cost accumulated over the years he worked on his dream. Yet, despite the low funds, he never stopped improving; each failed test was an opportunity to learn how *not* to do it.

d. The first success is not the final: There were several instances when the rockets seemed to be working fine. However, these were prototypes at best. Musk recorded this first success as a catalyst for other successes, and this is a big lesson for building big ideas. The first level is not the final level. It is a journey.

e. Share your ideas and ask for feedback: This was exactly what Elon Musk did after the first successes and failures. He consulted more and let experts provide guidance. When you are working with a big idea, you will always need help in terms of knowledge sharing and feedback. Do not do it all alone.

Sustainable Consolidation: Building Something That Lasts: Building something is one thing; building something that outlasts you is another. I've had to let go of some projects in my life because, although I could complete them now, they wouldn't remain relevant for long. I'm more focused on creating something that will have a lasting impact, and you should be too. The world needs to think long-term, not just short-term, so we can all make meaningful contributions. The work will feel more worthwhile when we consider the sacrifices made to build it. It's essential to remember that our legacy should address a relevant human need. Additionally, as we build, we must always plan for succession. It's important to prepare for what happens after we're gone.

The Creator's Paradox: Balancing Perfectionism and Progress: I have struggled with perfectionism for most of my life. It was in my research for this book that I found out that it is quite common to find this issue of perfectionism in people who are success-driven. The desire to build for the long term may cause one to focus on the project being perfect in every way, and when this pursuit of perfection gets in the way of the building, we still tend to stop the building because of a few hitches that may not even matter. However, there will always be second editions, and sometimes even third and fourth. This teaches us that progress is more important than perfection. So long as you keep improving, you will find success, with or without perfection. The discovery of antibiotics was one of the greatest creations of human history, but it was stumbled upon rather than perfectly planned out. Every creator must overcome this malady of always wanting everything to be so precise and pure. The journey to building a legacy will be fraught with diverse mistakes and imperfections, and the creator must be flexible enough to adapt, improve, and keep building.

6. Conception: Birth of New Possibilities

When Jeff Bezos first pitched the idea of an online bookstore, many doubted its potential. The internet was still in its infancy, and few could imagine a future where people would prefer to shop online. But Bezos saw an opportunity that others didn't. With a vision of building the world's most customer-centric company, he launched Amazon from his garage, setting the stage for a revolution in retail. The journey wasn't easy. Skepticism surrounded the idea of an internet marketplace, and early struggles threatened to derail his vision. However, Bezos remained steadfast, focusing relentlessly on innovation and customer experience. He didn't just want to sell books—he wanted to create a platform where customers could find anything they needed, at the best prices, with unmatched convenience. The dream he conceived as a young man eventually bloomed greater than his imagination. Amazon expanded beyond books, introducing features like one-click shopping, personalized recommendations, and fast delivery, setting new industry standards. Despite criticism and market fluctuations, Bezos kept pushing forward, reinvesting profits into innovations like Amazon Prime, cloud computing, and even artificial intelligence. Today, Amazon is more than just a retail giant—it's also a symbol of how bold ideas can change the world.

Life, as we know it, begins with conception. Just as it works in the conception of a human embryo, every great possibility starts with conception, a deliberate process that creates innovations, shifts mindsets, and builds a future. Yet, it is not enough to remain at the conceptual level of things. We must design strategies that will turn possibilities into realities. How can this be achieved?

Incubating Game-Changing Ideas: Techniques from Great Innovators: Innovation occurs through step-wise action plans that start from the abstract idea to life-changing discoveries. Like the great innovators of the past, from Leonardo da Vinci to Steve Jobs, each industry giant had strateg es that worked for them, and fortunately for us, most of these strategies are similar. I have studied several great innovators, and this list is a confluence of all their processes and techniques:

1. Question Everything. It is not creative to be satisfied with longstanding traditions; dig deeply into problems and challenge assumptions. *Why do we do this? Can I find a new way to achieve this?*

2. Be intentional in seeking ideas: Yes, inspiration for innovative ideas can come on its own, but great innovators go out in search of problems to solve. *How do I make life better for everyone? What are the needs I must solve?*

3. Work in the right environment: To brainstorm novel ideas and make great discoveries, all great innovators work in places that foster original thinking. Marie Curie lived in her lab, while Michelangelo was famous for sitting for long hours in open gardens and parks. Is your environment supportive of your dreams?

4. Embrace failure and learn from it: Like Reed Hastings, approach every failure as a step towards ultimate success. I do not see failure as an opportunity to quit, but rather as an insight into what works.

5. Resilience is key: Every innovation will encounter several battles along the way. You might get ridiculed for challenging the status quo, and you may lack support. But none of these is a reason to quit. Walt Disney had a great imagination, but he could overcome setbacks that brought him to the forefront of global entertainment.

From Nikola Tesla to Maya Lin, every great innovator is an individual who started small, brainstormed daily, sought solutions to diverse needs, and was comfortable with failure. Embracing these habits will bring life to our ideas.

From Imagination to Innovation: Bridging the Gap: I cannot count how many ideas, stories, and plans have formed in my head in the last ten years and remained as imagination and ideas to date. This is not a challenge peculiar to me. Everyone has, at one time or the other, come up with a brilliant idea that was never acted upon. So what makes the difference? How did the innovators convert their concepts into reality? Three things: Structure, discipline, and action. A structure is a laid-out plan including steps on how to move from a great vision in the mind to the actual work that is done. Then, there is the place of being disciplined enough to move beyond the ideation stage and execute the steps in the structure. Finally, having taken the first steps, there is a need to put these designs into action, decisions, and tasks. These are the things that separate the great innovators from the great idealists. Once we can build experiments with prototypes, we will have achieved more than most people can only imagine.

Conceptual Thinking: Seeing Patterns and Connections: Many events unfold in our lifetime, and we encounter numerous people, places, and experiences. However, only a few individuals develop the mindset of seeking commonalities among the diverse elements they encounter. This is the foundation of conceptual thinking: the ability to recognize relationships among separate pieces of information and organize them into a unified framework. This skill, shared by great scientists and leaders, allows us to understand complex systems, devise innovative solutions, see the bigger picture, and predict future outcomes. It's important to note that this skill can be learned through deliberate practice and techniques.

a. Seek to understand and ask questions about processes.
b. Pay attention to changes and analyze trends.
c. Use analogies in speeches and studies to find similarities and differences.
d. Gain knowledge across different fields outside your scope.
e. Train the mind to consistently consider different perspectives. Once the brain is trained to think unconventionally and discover trends in unrelated problems, it becomes easy to adopt solutions from one field and apply them to another sphere of life.

The Ethics of Creation: Responsible Innovation: When Albert Einstein and other scientists worked on the groundbreaking "equation of life and death," they could never have anticipated that their discovery would later become an instrument for the most devastating destruction in human history. Many innovators throughout history have found themselves on the wrong side of progress, despite their remarkable inventions, because their creations were either misused or not designed with humanity's well-being in mind. While these issues can be philosophical, ethics and kindness are essential in ensuring that our innovations have a positive impact on the world. Every creator must take responsibility for protecting their inventions from exploitation or harm. With growing concerns over privacy, misinformation on social media, and the rise of artificial intelligence, there's an increasing call for a global regulatory body to ensure innovations remain aligned with the greater good. By prioritizing ethical standards in our work, we can build a legacy that encourages positive development and progress for humanity.

CHAPTER 3

Communication:
Bridging Worlds

"To effectively communicate, we must realize that we are all different in the way we perceive the world and use this understanding as a guide to our communication with others."
—Tony Robbins

For centuries, Egyptian hieroglyphs remained an unsolvable mystery—an ancient language frozen in time, with no key to unlock its meaning. All that changed with the discovery of the Rosetta Stone in 1799. This single artifact, inscribed with the same text in three different scripts—Greek, Demotic (ancient Egyptian cursive), and hieroglyphs—provided the breakthrough scholars needed to finally decode a lost language and reconnect with a civilization long past. The Rosetta Stone went from being a fascinating linguistic puzzle to being a bridge between cultures and eras. By deciphering its inscriptions, scholars unlocked the secrets of Egyptian writing and gained deeper insights into their history, beliefs, and way of life. This is one of the biggest testaments to the power of communication—the ability to preserve knowledge, convey meaning, and bring different worlds together. This discovery underscores the importance of clear and effective communication. Whether between ancient civilizations or modern societies, the ability to share and understand information shapes our progress.

However, it must be said that the nuance of communication is such that words can mean entirely different things to two different people because of past experiences or a simple lack of clarity. It is possible to have the best intentions and still communicate wrongly because communication is not only about speaking a language you understand, but also about speaking a language that the other person can comprehend. Mistakes happen when communication is unclear. Relationships are broken, opportunities are missed, and it becomes even more impossible to bridge gaps the wider the communication gap gets.

Most of my career has been spent in enrollment management, and I have discovered that there is often a singular difference between candidates accepted into our institutions and those who were denied. It is just a single word: Communication. From writing essays and statements of purpose to sitting in front of a panel, answering questions, a major factor that distinguishes the best candidates is the ability to correctly communicate their strengths and convince the admissions board. This is why I have always coached people to embrace becoming lifelong learners and continuously improve. During the past two decades of my career as an enrollment manager, I have observed firsthand the complex challenges that multiple institutions face in trying to bridge this communication gap between management and staff, academic staff and students, and student-to-student, Nations have gone to war over simple miscommunication, and it is no wonder that modern higher education is not considered complete without fine-tuning the communication skills of their students.

1. Clarity: Cutting Through The Noise

The first "C" under communication is clarity. That fine art of making your message so clear and easy to understand that it becomes impossible to misunderstand. It is the art of eliminating ambiguity and ensuring that anyone who hears or sees your message understands what you mean to communicate. But how do you do this? How do you break down complex ideas into easy-to-digest chunks?

There's something that usually happens to me when I have an idea. It sounds so brilliant in my head that I assume anybody with a brain would be able to understand what I intend to communicate. Because of this, whenever I was not understood, I always concluded that it had more to do with the listener than it had to do with me. But I was wrong. As I would later find out, it was *my* fault if I communicated an idea and nobody understood me. I was the one who was communicating incorrectly. I was the one who had failed to present my idea in a way that the other party could understand. I was the one who was a bad communicator. It had little to do with the other party.

The goal of any communication should be to break it down so clearly that even a five-year-old can understand what you're trying to say. Astrophysics is a subject filled with mind-bending concepts—black holes, dark matter, and the vastness of the universe. To many, these ideas seem distant and incomprehensible. However, Neil deGrasse Tyson has spent his career making them accessible, using simple analogies and engaging storytelling to bridge the gap between scientific complexity and everyday understanding. Instead of overwhelming audiences with equations and technical jargon, Tyson paints vivid pictures with words. He compares the warping of space-time to placing a heavy object on a trampoline, illustrating how gravity works. He likens the vast number of stars in the universe to the grains of sand on Earth's beaches, helping people grasp the sheer scale of the cosmos. Through television appearances, books, and speeches, Tyson has turned astrophysics into something relatable and exciting. His approach highlights that communication isn't just about knowledge—it's about connection. Tyson's ability to make people care about the universe underscores the power of clear, engaging communication. By transforming complex science into compelling stories, his style has shown that the most profound ideas can inspire anyone, regardless of their background.

Distilling complex ideas requires you to think of your audience first. For example, if you're speaking to a five-year-old, you want to think of things they can relate to and use that to draw up analogies to pass across your message. If you're speaking to a group of scientists, you want to connect your ideas to things they might relate better with, like using the fluidity of water to describe the flow of money. However, the general rule is to ALWAYS KEEP IT SIMPLE.

I usually use the **T.A.R.G.E.T**. framework to help me tailor my message for my audience.

T - Type of Audience: If my audience is executives, I know my message must get to the point immediately. If I have a general audience, I must mix the things I refer to or the analogies I make to get the point across to different people simultaneously.

A - Align to the Goal: Here, I'm always thinking of what I want my audience to think, feel, or do after hearing my message. My message when I want to merely inform is completely different when I want to inspire action, even if I might be talking about the same thing. For example, "Happy times spent with family directly correlate with personal satisfaction" differs from "Spend at least 30 minutes a day with your family if you want to increase your satisfaction." The same message is passed in two different ways according to my goal.

R- Refine the Message: Simplify, structure, and organize your content so it's easy to understand. I use the What → Why → How method by asking myself: What is the big idea? Why is it relevant to this particular audience? How does it work? This way, I can cut out the unnecessary parts of my message and stick to only what is needed.

G - Gather the Right Tools: It is very easy to ignore the place of communication tools, that is, tools that help you make your message easier to understand. For example, holding up a picture pointing to the left communicates to my audience that they must go left without me saying a word. Always find tools that can make your message easier to understand.

E- Engage the Audience: I've never been in a room where I didn't feel a subconscious need to feel seen or like my presence mattered. It's why a particular side of the room lights up when a comedian shares a joke that has context unique to their culture, and why we all feel good when a friend reminds us of something we had taught them before. People like to feel seen.

When communicating, we must ensure that our message considers this. Ask yourself: What stories or metaphors will my audience relate to? At what point should I insert a question in my presentation to have the audience interact? Can I help my child understand why I want her to do a particular thing by sharing a story of why it means so much to me?

T- Test for Understanding: One of the best ways to refine methods and strategies for communication is to test them. Find ways to practice all you learn about communication, and refine it based on how your audience reacts and responds.

Frameworks and strategies are useful pillars of communication until you have to communicate under pressure. It is hard to remember what you are supposed to do when emotions are high or when it is a high-stakes situation. However, that doesn't mean you're supposed to just "wing it" in those times. We need communication strategies even more when we're under pressure. What makes a negotiator worth their salt, for example, is how they manage high-pressure situations instead of giving in to pressure. To be a great communicator, one must learn the art of clarity in crisis.

The first thing to do in high-pressure situations is to *listen* instead of trying to talk. High-pressure situations are diffused much faster when you understand the other party and can connect with what they're saying. So, listen to seek clarity on where the other person is at. It is through listening and noticing body cues that you can understand the other party's true motivation. Once you understand their motivation, you're halfway through communicating.

2. **Collaboration**: Synergy in Action

Is competition for losers? Peter Thiel's bold claim challenges much of what we've been taught about the value of competition. While we're often told that competition pushes us to improve and perform at our best, what's rarely acknowledged is that our individual capacity has limits. If collaboration is an available option and I still choose competition, then I may be missing out on far more than I gain. I see collaboration as a powerful force—one that multiplies opportunities and helps overcome individual weaknesses. In many cases, working together can achieve more than going it alone.

This is how I see it. Every human being or institution has to deal with the natural order that states that where we have certain strengths, there are bound to be weaknesses, too. That is limiting even for the best of us. However, collaboration brings a twist where Party B's strength covers Party A's weakness, and Party C's strength is amplified by Parties A and B. It is very difficult to lose when you have a collaboration that works. This is where teamwork comes in.

Collaboration on a larger scale — merging companies, making peace with competitors, and so on — will be stunted if internal collaboration is not functional. But how are high-performance teams built? The first rule of thumb is to create synergy. That means ensuring the team members understand that what they do for others uplifts them, and what they do for themselves uplifts others. That creates a symbiotic relationship where each team member begins to watch their counterpart's back because they know one man down means the whole team is stunted. This kind of mindset can take a team from one to a hundred because instead of being a competition where the fight is about "Who's better than who?" it becomes a collaboration about "How can we work together to achieve the best results for us all?"

I experienced the effects of both mindsets while leading a team during the initial stages of my career. When it was a competition, one person always wanted to do better than the others in pursuit of higher remuneration or benefits. However, while one person delivered great work, others did not, affecting the overall output. Additionally, the innate nature of competition that tempts the competitive party into sabotage severely limits the team's abilities. When we moved to the synergy model, each team member seemed to figure out that they could only win if they used their strengths to cover the other person's weaknesses and allowed others to do the same for them. In this model, team members thought of ways to help their teammates, and overall goals were being met.

To master the art of collaboration, we must break down silos. Teams within organizations shouldn't operate in isolation but should align their efforts toward a common objective. This may involve forming cross-functional teams that bring together members from different departments to focus on a specific goal. More importantly, it requires removing communication barriers and promoting transparency. Doing so helps build a collective mindset—one where everyone understands they're working toward the same purpose.

This cross-functional approach also works when it has to do with two entirely different organizations. The secret lies in finding a shared goal. For example, a company that manufactures hearing aids should not feel threatened by a research company working to find a way to cure deafness. Their shared goal is clear — to give people who would otherwise have no chance of hearing a chance to hear. If these companies could communicate and find this common ground, they would find more advantages in collaborating than competing.

This also applies to the family. Most arguments would be eliminated if the family members realized they are a unit and embraced a collaborative mindset. It would even change communication because the question would go from an aggressive "How are *you* going to solve this?" to a more considerate "How are *we* going to solve this?"

3. Connection: The Human Touch in a Digital World

There's a current craze to network in professional settings today. It probably stems from the fact that we've been told that the quality of the people we know helps us as we climb the proverbial career ladder. It's true to an extent — the people in your life greatly impact who you are and who you have the potential to become. Perhaps this is why it's a mistake to treat people as just contacts instead of building valuable relationships that could greatly impact our lives.

What is the difference between building a repertoire of contacts and building relationships? One difference is that you cannot have as many relationships as you have contacts. Relationships are intentional and value-driven instead of parasitic. In relationships, you aren't just trying to ensure you have someone who might put in a good word for you somewhere; you're acknowledging the real value of the human you're interacting with and ensuring you treat them with respect while thinking of ways to add value to their lives.

It has certainly felt cathartic for me to attend an event and get the cards of the highest players in the room. However, if I were being realistic with myself, what did that do for me apart from the euphoria of that moment? It was odd and did not work out when I tried to ask for a favor from someone just because I had their card. However, when I changed my strategy and decided to focus on connecting with people because I could see myself offering them value or pursuing a longer mutually beneficial relationship with them, the results changed.

Of course, it was harder — being intentional is not a walk in the park — but it helped me forge deeper connections, even while building myself up due to the exchange of value in these relationships. There's a reason we cannot connect to everybody. For two or more people to connect, they must have something in common, and I don't mean their attributes must be the same. Rather, when you see two people connect, it is because they have shared values or goals. The random friend you connect so well with, even though you seemingly have nothing in common, is your friend because there's something you both like talking about, something you both enjoy doing, and so on.

Connection is like a thread that binds, and it cannot exist if there is no thread. Even two people with completely opposing views can build a relationship because they both like having someone with a different view to debate issues with. That's the thread. Does this mean that a connection automatically happens because we share values with someone or have a "thread" with someone? Of course not. Sometimes, connections happen because of what scientists call the "mere exposure" effect. The more you are in proximity to someone, the more you bond with them. Other times, they trigger an empathetic response in you, and you feel drawn to them.

There are many reasons why connections happen, but what's universal is that the human psyche was made for interaction and connection. We must be deliberate about fostering relationships that go deep. Here are some tips that may help:

1. **Build Familiarity:** When you meet someone, be intentional about spending consistent time together to build trust and comfort.
2. **Find Common Ground:** Look for shared values, interests, or experiences.
3. **Engage in Co-Creation**: Collaborate on activities or projects to deepen emotional ties. This is also one way you can ensure that there is a value exchange.
4. **Understand Personality Differences:** Adapt to others' connection styles (e.g., introverts vs. extroverts).
5. **Balance Individuality and Belonging**: While people need to feel part of a group, they also value being seen as unique individuals. This is especially helpful when you go to events where everyone is assumed to like one particular thing.

In recent times, relationship building and connection have taken another form. You can befriend someone you've never met, connect with a mentor you've always admired, or build relationships with someone from a different continent. That's the power technology, especially via social media platforms, has given us. And while I think the power of social media in building connections should be considered the world's eighth wonder, I am also concerned about the misuse of this great gift.

With social media decentralizing access and making it incredibly easy to approach anyone, we must remember that the rules of boundaries and basic respect haven't changed. Approach people online like you would approach someone in front of you — with respect and courtesy. Present yourself as you would if you were in an important event, with the understanding that people are forming perceptions about you, and how you communicate your value is how other people perceive you. Never become careless or unintentional on social media.

Additionally, as you build global relationships through social media or travel, endeavor to learn the other party's culture. It communicates respect and a sense of value if you can relate to someone from a different culture based on their culture. That always leaves an impression. Connections are how the world goes around. Make the most of it.

4. Consensus: The Art of Agreement

I used to think that discussions, especially in challenging or high-stakes environments, were about winning—getting my point across louder, clearer, and more convincingly than the other side. It didn't take me long to realize how hollow that "win" felt when the room was tense, and the solution we reached seemed like everyone had been forced. Productive discussions are never easy. They require intentionality, patience, and skill—qualities that master mediators use to make the most of every discussion. Mediators know that their role isn't to fix problems for people but to help participants uncover shared ground, clarify misunderstandings, and co-create a way forward. Here's what I have learned from observing and applying their techniques:

Set the Right Tone Early

Master mediators set the ground rules early: respect, active listening, and open-mindedness. They frame the discussion as a joint pursuit of a solution rather than a battle to win. I found that by starting with, "We're all here to figure this out together," the energy in the room softened, and people leaned in rather than bracing themselves for a fight.

Listen to Understand, Not to Respond

We've all been guilty of it: nodding while someone talks but already rehearsing what we'll say next. Master mediators do something different—they truly listen. They allow silence after someone speaks, giving time for their thoughts to land, and they repeat key points to ensure they understand the other person well. They might say, "What I hear you saying is…" This kind of listening makes people feel heard and often de-escalates tension. I tried it once in a particularly heated meeting and was amazed at how much it shifted the tone. Listening with intention allowed me to see where people were coming from rather than where I thought they were.

Find the Thread of Agreement

Discussions often go off the rails because we focus on differences rather than shared goals. Master mediators are skilled at uncovering common ground, even during disagreements. For example, two team members may have opposing ideas, but both care deeply about the project's success. Pointing this out, "It's clear you both want what's best for this project; you just have different visions for how to get there," can shift the focus from conflict to collaboration. Finding this thread required me to ask better questions, like: "What matters most to us?" What are we trying to achieve together?"

Address Emotions, Not Just Logic

When people feel dismissed, the fire of disagreement burns hotter because they want to defend themselves even more. So, master mediators have learned the art of addressing emotions head-on. By naming the emotion in the room, they give people permission to release it, which clears the path for a productive conversation.

Ask Open-Ended Questions

Nobody wants to be told what to do, and it is far better to allow a person to solve for themselves rather than spoon-feed them what you think they should do. Master mediators uphold this by asking open-ended questions that lead the parties to workable solutions. They ask questions like, "What would an ideal outcome look like for you?" or "What's one step we can agree on to move forward?" I once spent over 30 minutes debating a minor issue in a team meeting—until I asked, "What's the simplest way to resolve this?" Suddenly, everyone stopped arguing and started thinking about my question.

The fact is that there are many times when everyone in the room will not have the same stance, and that's completely okay. What matters is finding that point where both parties can agree, and being willing to let go of the things that matter to you when it doesn't resonate with everyone else. However, while we certainly need consensus in situations where decisions affect everyone or when it has to do with long-term relationships and shared goals, there are times when consensus should not be pursued.

For example, in cases where executives need to make decisions quickly, it can be a waste of time to ask everyone in the organization what they think. In cases like this, these quick decisions should be influenced by already-established values and procedures in the organization. Another situation I experienced firsthand is the downfall of seeking consensus when expertise should lead instead. Trying to get the consensus of the marketing and social media team for something that requires IT support doesn't pay off. These decisions can be made excellently by deferring to the person with the most knowledge of the subject.

Another pitfall I avoid when seeking consensus is the danger of groupthink, or a situation where no one is willing to take responsibility for a situation because they're just going with what everybody else is saying. In moments like this, I emphasize to my team that consensus doesn't mean shutting down unique ideas; rather, it means discovering how several unique ideas can work together for optimal results.

In environments where viewpoints differ, consensus might look like agreeing to do it a certain way this time and another way next time. I have learned that when people cannot agree or share no common ground, it is best to let results do the talking.

5. Conveyance: Mastering the Message

The ability to tell a story holds immense power to change the world. Stories can shift perspectives, challenge long-held beliefs, and reshape the way we see others. For example, I might feel anger when I hear a news report about a robbery—until I learn that the person involved was a 21-year-old mother of three, driven by desperation to save her dying child. Stories create understanding. I often say that something may seem bad or inexcusable—until someone tells a story that helps us see the human side of it.

If stories have this much power, it is a mistake to ignore them when we are trying to craft narratives that could change the world for good. Always have a good story. It doesn't have to be false. It should just be excellent at paying attention and finding ways to connect the most random things to buttress your point. Nobody might remember an ad about a vet down the street, but they will remember an ad that tells the story about how the vet saved a beloved dog's life, only to find that the dog was an older woman's companion, and the vet had inadvertently saved both the dog and the older woman.

Stories have a way of sticking, so I always make it a point to communicate my message by adding a story that illustrates the point I'm trying to make while also making an impact in my listener's mind. But storytelling is not the only hack to better communication. You must also be aware of the message you send with your body, microexpressions that flit across your face, and your gestures.

Many people assume that only body language experts can accurately interpret microexpressions. While experts may have a deeper understanding, it's important to realize that others can still *sense* what your body language, gestures, or facial expressions are communicating—even if they can't fully explain why. Here's a key lesson I've learned about communication: if someone senses that I don't mean what I'm saying, or if my body language sends a message of indifference, I've already lost them. People respond to what they feel, not just what they hear.

Communication has a lot to do with trust, and you cannot pass on a message when the other person is inclined to doubt whatever you say. We're often unaware that we are passing messages with our bodies or facial expressions, even when we mean whatever it is we are saying. To improve at communication, I realize that I have the responsibility to ensure that what I'm saying *without* words aligns with what I'm saying *with* my words. Here are some non-verbal cues I've mastered to ensure I'm passing the message across excellently:

1. **Posture and Presence:** I learned that how I carry myself determines people's perception of me. Stand tall, avoid slouching, and ensure an open posture to signal your authority and full attention.
2. **Eye Contact:** Too little feels evasive; too much feels aggressive. I learned to strike a balance—meeting people's eyes when making key points, then naturally breaking contact to maintain comfort.
3. **Gestures and Hands**: I often keep my hands visible, avoiding "pocket hiding" or fidgeting, which can make my audience believe I'm unsure of what I'm saying.

Appropriate hand gestures also reinforce my words by emphasizing and clarifying my message.

4. **Tone:** A slow, deliberate tone emphasizes the importance of my message, and changing my pitch helps to keep the audience engaged.

> One thing I've learned to always keep in mind is that effective communication—and mastering how to share a message—comes with the power to influence others. That's a responsibility I don't take lightly. Persuasion doesn't mean pressuring someone to agree with you; it involves helping them understand why something is valuable or beneficial to them.
>
> When I need to persuade or influence someone in this way, I start by building credibility. People don't listen to someone they don't trust, and I've realized that I'm responsible for earning that trust. That's why I make sure my message is truthful, supported by facts, and something I'm personally willing to stand behind. This is also where I rely on data to strengthen my message. By breaking down complex information and presenting it clearly, I help my audience see exactly why I believe in what I'm saying.

We often think an audience will get confused by data, but that is not always true. They are interested in the evidence but can't comprehend the statistics and numbers without help. So, to ensure clarity, I have learned to turn numbers into a story. For example, instead of saying, "The data shows that 80% of people quit after a month at the gym", I would say, "Even though evidence shows that only 2 out of 10 people continue going to the gym after one month, this is because they don't break down their fitness goals into easily achievable chunks. So, when Maria doesn't see any improvement after one month, she quits. The same happens with Sam, Cheryl, and Barry."

What I have done with this example is add context to what was previously a piece of bland data to show my audience how they have been doing it wrong. We must master how to convey our message so we don't leave the audience confused, bored, and without clarity or action points.

6. Charisma: Inspiring Others to Action

It's tempting to think charisma is an inborn trait — something you have or don't. But the truth is that charisma can be learned. I used to assume that people with a magnetic presence were just "naturals," born with the gift of effortlessly drawing others to them. Yet, when I began to observe them closely, I realized that charisma comes from deliberate practice. It's about how you carry yourself, engage others, and the energy you bring to the room.

For example, I noticed that the large presence charismatic people have is just them displaying the art of being fully in the moment. They listen intently, and they make others feel seen. They have a special way of not dominating the conversation but inviting others into it so that they know that what they have to say is important, too. The second thing charismatic people get right is confidence without arrogance. They have a sense of certainty in what they say, which shows in how they say it. They can hold eye contact without making it uncomfortable, speak clearly, and exude calm even when things feel chaotic.

These elements of charisma are all things that can be learned and practiced, but I always had to remind myself that trying to be charismatic didn't mean copying others, but being authentic. I had to learn to be uniquely myself even while applying the principles of charisma I had learned. I used to try to emulate leaders I admired. Perhaps I felt that if I could look like them, make jokes like them, and imitate their posture and pitch, I would give off the same aura that they did. But that failed woefully. I couldn't seamlessly be another person, no matter how much I tried, but what I could always be was myself.

True charisma happens when I lean into my strengths and unashamedly communicate from a place of integrity. When we think of someone we admire, we find that what makes them compelling is not the fact that they are flashy or perfect. It's likely their realness — their ability to share a story with vulnerability, to admit mistakes, or to champion something they believe in that makes them so inspiring.

Authenticity creates trust, and trust is magnetic. Something shifted when I stopped trying to be "more charismatic" and instead focused on sharing my values and engaging people with genuine curiosity. However, there's a fine line between influence and exploitation. That's why balancing charisma with integrity is so critical. We always need to ask ourselves if we're being charismatic to toot our horns, or to help others. I found that when my intentions were aligned with something bigger than my gain, for example, helping my team succeed, my influence carried weight. And that was because I made sure I wasn't utilizing my charm and poise to manipulate others.

But there are other ways to misuse charisma beyond manipulation. Early in my career, I gave a presentation to an international audience. I relied on my usual style — expressive gestures, enthusiastic storytelling — only to notice that some attendees seemed reserved and distant. Later, I found out why. In some cultures, subtlety and humility are more respected than overt confidence. I failed to understand that charisma is about reading the room and discerning the values and communication styles of the people you engage with so you can adapt accordingly.

In Japan, for example, I learned that active listening and measured pauses convey respect and dignity. Meanwhile, a more assertive and engaging delivery usually resonates in the United States. I'm not saying you have to abandon your authenticity; you do have to be dynamic enough to adjust your expression of it.

CHAPTER 4

Change:
Navigating the Winds of Transformation

"Progress is impossible without change, and those who cannot change their minds cannot change anything."
—George Bernard Shaw

1.2 billion. That's how many lives will forever change due to the unprecedented use of workplace automation technologies in the coming decade. Nearly everyone will feel the impact: from young graduates embarking on their careers to working professionals in need of reskilling and upskilling. Learning and adaptation are the only ways that we can tackle this challenge and maintain our relevance in the future workplace. We must all become lifelong learners—and we must continuously improve. The workplace of the future will be starkly different from that of the Industrial Revolution, and this is why higher education institutions are striving to transform their study curricula to reflect this new era.

During the past two decades of my career as an enrollment manager, I have observed firsthand the complex challenges that multiple institutions face in trying to bridge this gap for their students. This is why Excelerate was born. Excelerate is a unique technology platform that empowers learners of all backgrounds with experiential learning opportunities, enabling them to gain the competencies and skills necessary to thrive in the twenty-first-century job market. I hope that this revolutionizes education as we know it, but we must first learn to embrace change.

The one constant thing in life is change. Strangely, it is also the one thing we are most afraid of. This is because when change comes, it is usually painful or so different that we are tempted to shy away. I understand well what that fear can be like. I experienced an enormous change at a time that was supposed to be the happiest in my life. I was starting on a path many would have killed for, but all I could think about was my doubts about meeting all the position's requirements. I had never been challenged in that way before, and I almost allowed the fear to stop me from embracing the change that would, in a few years, put me on a path to the greatest privileges and opportunities in my life.

If we see change as the wind that blows us toward transformation, it will become easier to welcome it, even if everything initially appears tumultuous. There's so much waiting at the end of the unfamiliar, but if we insist on staying in familiar places, we might never get to experience the other things that life can offer.

1. Challenges: Embracing the Uncomfortable

Are you familiar with the story of Netflix? When Reed Hastings co-founded Netflix, he didn't just change how people watch movies—he revolutionized an entire industry. The company initially started as a DVD rental service, competing with giants like Blockbuster. However, Hastings had a bigger vision. He saw a future where entertainment was streamed instantly, anywhere, without the need for physical media. Many doubted the idea, but he remained committed to transforming the way people experienced entertainment. The transition wasn't easy. Early on, streaming technology was limited, and internet speeds were a major barrier. Investors were skeptical, and traditional media companies underestimated the potential of digital platforms. But Hastings persisted, constantly improving Netflix's streaming capabilities and expanding its content library. His focus on user experience— offering on-demand access, personalized recommendations, and original programming—set Netflix apart. It was an uncomfortable journey filled with several failures and challenges, but Netflix didn't just survive the shift to streaming—it led it. The company pioneered binge-watching, changed how TV shows are produced, and became a dominant force in the entertainment world. By continually adapting and staying ahead of trends, Netflix grew into a global leader, proving that bold vision and persistence can reshape an entire industry. The story of Netflix is the story of change, and Hastings's success shows that the future belongs to those willing to challenge the status quo, take risks, and keep innovating, no matter the obstacles.

From this story, I learned to see every obstacle or failure as a way to pass through instead of as a stop sign. If I have problems with my team members? I take it as a sign that there are structures that I haven't yet set in place. If I can't reach my goals? I understand it is a capacity problem, a time problem, or a knowledge gap, not because I am a failure. So, the obstacle to my failed goals is only telling me to expand my capacity by practice, give it more time, or increase my knowledge.

If we were to think this way about every problem, it would be hard to remain in despair for long. Our minds begin to think of a way out of the problem, instead of being afraid that the problem is too big to surmount. This is usually the bedrock of any change — the willingness to embrace what is uncomfortable and let it lead you to transformation. Sometimes, the roadblock you encounter isn't meant to stop you; it's meant to redirect or force you to innovate. The greatest breakthroughs often emerge because someone refuses to see a challenge as the final word.

When we think about it, history has proven this time and again. Entire companies, movements, and individuals have thrived because they adopted what we now call a "growth mindset"—the belief that challenges aren't meant to define you. They are there to help you grow. Having a growth mindset is essential for making any positive change. If you believe there's only one path to your goal, you'll likely get stuck when that path doesn't work out. But with a growth mindset, you're open to exploring new strategies and finding alternative ways to reach your goal. Everyone who has achieved greatness—the "hall of fame" achievers—got there because they embraced change, welcomed innovation, saw old problems in new ways, and weren't afraid to challenge the status quo.

However, there's a catch. While challenging the status quo, breaking barriers, and finding new ways to do things signal transformation, I discovered that if I did not learn the magic of timing and necessity, I would only be rocking the boat to prove a point rather than bringing about positive change. Before I challenge what has always been done, I ask myself, *"What outcome am I trying to achieve?" "Is this challenge constructive or disruptive for the sake of disruption?"*

We should never do things without a properly defined objective, but neither should we give up when it can bring transformation, because everybody else insists it has always been done in a certain way. Here are some pointers that show it is time to do things differently:

- The current system no longer works
- You have evidence for a better way
- Innovation or growth is stagnant

2. Catalyst: Sparking Transformation

Change is difficult to initiate because it often needs someone bold enough to challenge what is and brave enough to inspire what could be. That's what a catalyst is — someone who drives transformation and change instead of waiting for it to happen. However, being a change agent doesn't just happen. I discovered that no one listens to or looks up to you until you have shown that change is possible by what you exemplify in how you handle things.

And that's the first strategy for driving any organizational shift. You must first become what you want to see, The next step is to develop a compelling vision. No footballer can score a goal without seeing the goalpost, and in the same way, we cannot expect change if we haven't defined what we intend to achieve. Another important factor is whether the people you want to transform are change-ready. Look for the ones who are, and start with them. That helps to build momentum and influence the people who are not yet ready.

A popular saying claims that little drops of water can make a mighty ocean, and I might be tempted to challenge the truth of that statement, seeing as an ocean contains a tremendous amount of water! However, I experienced the truth of this idea firsthand with a cause that was so dear to my heart. At first, it seemed impossible to raise the kind of funds that I needed to cover costs and make the impact that I wanted to make, and it was very tempting to conclude that I would never see the vision I had become a reality. However, I decided to do what I could with what I had, and what I had was enough funds and friends to help only one person. Even as I did the best I could at the time, I struggled to believe it was enough, but I continued in that way, helping one person at a time.

After five months of doing what looked "small" and being unable to see how I could get to the place where I envisioned, I received a call from someone who wanted to fund my cause. When I asked him how he knew about me, he shared that he'd encountered the first person I'd decided to start with. That person had shared the story of how I had helped them become better. He was calling after getting my number because he was very impressed that someone could be passionate about a cause and willing to do the best they could.

I learned then that little drops of water *can* make a mighty ocean, not because we have to wait for enough drops to fill the ocean, but because the little drops can cause a ripple effect. Imagine little drops of water beating steadily on a rock, and building a pool of water that causes the rock to shift and let loose the mighty river of water it had been holding back. That is exactly how ripple effects work. The small things gain momentum until they trigger something that causes a maximum overflow. After that experience, I never underestimated the power of small changes to drive big results.

I also needed to learn to focus on the right things. Leverage is only possible when the lever is placed at the fulcrum. You can have maximum impact when you focus on the things that give you leverage. For example, if you're trying to influence a team to achieve a certain result, you obtain leverage and do it faster if you focus on interacting with the person who has the most influence within that team. Or, if I'm trying to solve a problem in an organization, I can do it more efficiently by focusing on the underlying causes — the root of the problem — instead of just the manifestation of the problem. Always find the fulcrum and work from there to inspire change.

3. Conviction: Unwavering in the Face of Doubt

Nobody admires a person who cannot take a stand. If I made a practice of changing my mind according to the amount of pressure I was under, I would never be respected or trusted. However, we shouldn't stay true to our beliefs because of what others might think of us; we should ideally do it because we're confident in who we are and firm enough to establish boundaries.

Every human being should have a value system. A value system comprises our beliefs, convictions, and identified boundaries. We must be willing to communicate these values regardless of what it might cost. I believe our values should be divided into permanent values, which don't change no matter the circumstance, and semi-permanent values, which can be adjusted based on the severity of the circumstance.

An example of a permanent value is a decision not to say foul words. Another is to treat people respectfully. In this case, no matter how angry or irritated you are, you choose to say firm but kind words and respect the other person, no matter who they are. On the other hand, a semi-permanent value might be a decision to be in bed by 09:00 PM every night. While it is important to you, you can decide to put it aside for a moment if your colleague has an accident and you have to see them, or if the whole team has to work through the night.

It is important to distinguish between these two because the goal is to stay true to yourself even when your values are challenged. Most of us have heard the story of Nelson Mandela. In a nation divided by apartheid, he refused to accept a world where people were judged by the color of their skin. His commitment to equality and human rights led him to challenge one of the most oppressive systems in history, even at great personal cost. For 27 years, he endured harsh conditions on Robben Island, yet his spirit remained unbroken. While behind bars, he became a symbol of hope, inspiring a global movement that demanded his release and the end of apartheid. When he finally walked free in 1990, Mandela did not seek revenge—he sought reconciliation. His leadership in dismantling apartheid and promoting unity led to his election as South Africa's first Black president in 1994. Mandela's story is a testament to the power of standing firm in one's beliefs. His unwavering dedication to justice reminds us that real change requires courage, patience, and the willingness to fight for what is right, no matter the cost.

We often think that sticking to our principles and convictions is just about us — perhaps that's why we are sometimes so quick to give in instead of holding our ground, but one person's conviction is more than able to spark change in the hearts of plenty of others. We inspire those who hear our stories of conviction and bravery and ensure they have the fuel to stand true to themselves. History is written with the ink of people who refused to sacrifice their convictions in the face of pressure — people like Nelson Mandela and Martin Luther King Jr., to name a few. The amazing part is that even if we do not change the course of the future as powerfully as they did, we can also influence positive change by standing firm on our principles.

However, staying true to a conviction does not mean it's unnecessary to be open to correction or learn more. I tell my team that even though holding firmly to conviction is admirable, when we receive evidence that our convictions are wrong, we must be humble enough to drop those convictions and adopt new ones. Again, I re-emphasize the need to divide your convictions into permanent and semi-permanent ones. The permanent ones are there forever. Nothing should change them because of the values to which they are attached, like respect for human life, honesty and fairness, and so on. The semi-permanent ones are the ones that can be changed if enough evidence is provided for a change.

A question I am often asked is, "How is conviction built?" The answer is quite simple, though not necessarily easy. Conviction is built when you discover what is important and necessary to live maximally. My convictions, for example, were built over time by the things I disliked seeing. I vowed to treat every human with respect, no matter what, because I saw how disrespect could eat away at a person's soul and make them unaware of their value. Experiences like this are the things that shape convictions, and we must become bold enough to take a step and fight the fight that will inevitably come when we define our convictions.

4. Circumstance: Mastering
Any Situation

Life is unpredictable. I learned this firsthand when I had to deal with back-to-back issues that were out of my control, and I was left wondering if I had done something wrong to trigger the continuous blows the universe kept dealing me. But that's life. It hits when you least expect it and seems to want to challenge you to a fight. We tend to give up during these times because we have no fight left in us. However, circumstances don't change until you do something about them. A circumstance can either evolve into an opportunity or a crisis, depending on how you deal with it.

Learning that I cannot always control the environment — how people behave, where the mistakes in my past led me, and so on-has changed my life for the better. I learned to figure out the parts of the environment that I couldn't control and adapt to them, and then take the parts that I can control and exert my authority over them. We need knowledge of how to adapt and how to exert authority to be able to thrive when things get unpredictable and shaky.

For example, I was once falsely accused by an individual and made to deal with the repercussions of something I hadn't done. I couldn't control the lies told about me, so I had to adapt quickly and think of whom I could call to defend me before things got out of hand. I couldn't control the person who had lied against me, but I could think quickly and work to ensure the situation did not escalate. I recognized that I could control how I reacted to the betrayal, and I chose to react calmly instead of with rage. I also chose to forgive and cut ties with the person afterward. This was me exerting my authority. We often have control over certain things, but do not take authority. Taking authority is recognizing that you have control and then taking the steps to control the situation. By choosing to forgive, I exercised my right not to have my mind and emotions weighed down by what someone else had chosen to do, and that helped me more than any fight could have.

Learn to stay calm in every circumstance that occurs. That's the only way to find a way out or make lemonade out of lemons. When I find that I can't stay calm, I allow myself to take a break from making any crucial decisions at that moment. If I can't think clearly, there can be no decisions made. This applies to both happy and sad circumstances. Happiness is one of the good emotions, but making decisions when I am overly happy might mean over-promising or saying things I cannot take responsibility for. Sadness or anger, on the other hand, might make me say something I don't mean and give away any leverage I have. That's why getting calm is always my first course of action. When I'm calm, I can read the situation well enough to see the opportunities or loopholes, and that's the only way I can stay on top of any circumstance.

Circumstantial intelligence is the ability to understand a situation quickly, recognize what's happening around you, and respond effectively. It combines awareness, adaptability, and clear decision-making to navigate any scenario, especially when circumstances are uncertain or constantly changing. The key here is learning to adjust your response based on what you notice about the environment, people, or general circumstances.

5. Contemplation: The Fuel for Evolution

Learn to ask questions, think things through, and reflect deeply—this habit leads to meaningful accomplishments. Critical thinking and contemplation are especially important because you can't change what you don't understand.

It always strikes me as odd when people follow trends or do things simply because it's what everyone else is doing. Just because something is popular doesn't make it right or worth doing.

Think back to our ancestors, who discovered how to make fire by striking two stones together. Have we ever stopped to wonder what would have happened if no one had been curious enough to question how things could be done differently? Even if that first spark was an accident, someone had to ask, "What caused it?" or "What materials were involved?" That curiosity and willingness to think critically is what (literally) sparked innovation in the first place.

Critical thinking and contemplation go beyond simply asking questions—they involve a continuous journey of uncovering the deeper layers of an issue. While questions are the gateway to discovery, not all questions are equally effective. To make meaningful progress, we must learn to ask the *right* questions.

So, what does a "right" question look like?

1. **A right question seeks understanding, not judgment.** It's open-ended and curious, not based on assumptions. For example, instead of asking, "Why do you always look so sad?" or "Why are you so lazy?"—which imply you already know what's wrong—it's more helpful to ask, "Is everything okay?" This invites honest expression and leaves room for the other person to share their perspective.

2. **A right question is specific.** Vague questions often lead to vague or confusing answers. If I'm curious about whether the Earth is round and I ask a scientist, "What can you tell me about the Earth?" I may get an overwhelming response that misses the point. But if I ask, "What can you tell me about the shape of the Earth?" I'm more likely to receive a clear, focused answer.

3. **A right question has a clear purpose.** Before asking, I need to understand *why* I'm asking. Am I trying to spark a new idea? Clarify a concept? Solve a problem? Knowing my objective helps me frame my question more effectively.

4. **The right question requires active listening.** If I'm not prepared to listen carefully, I'll likely miss important insights, ask poor follow-up questions, and come away no wiser. Listening is what transforms a question into a meaningful dialogue.

Overall, the right questions mostly feature a:

- **How** - to discern the process behind a phenomenon
- **Why** - to identify the cause and motivations

- **What** - to explore possibilities

When I meet a contemplative person, it tells me they are comfortable going beyond their comfort zone. They want to know what is out there and why, and it usually leads them to explore new horizons, say yes to new challenges, and, as a result, achieve so much more. This is why I intentionally encourage deep thinking in my teams. I ensure there's no judgment when they ask questions, and I reward attempts to experiment, even if they fail, and expose them to knowledge that challenges what they've always known.

Contemplation and critical thinking must be encouraged and practiced because it is the only way to innovate and sustain any real and positive change. Here are some tips I use to ensure I stay curious.

1. I've taught myself to always have a questioning mindset. I always ask, "Why?" and "What's next?"
2. I try to always learn something new, even if it means breaking it down into small, sizable chunks.
3. I seek feedback. Since I'm aware I don't know everything, I always grab an opportunity to gain insightful feedback.
4. I learn from others through mentorship, podcasts, books, and watching people I admire.

6. Constancy: The Backbone of Change

As beautiful as innovation, courage, creativity, and curiosity are, I've learned that they will not lead to positive change if I ignore the power of "keeping at it." It's one thing to identify something that needs to be done, another to start doing it, and another to make it non-negotiable. Non-negotiable goals are a declaration of intent, ones you refuse to compromise on regardless of setbacks or distractions. When you frame a goal as non-negotiable, your mindset shifts from "if" to "when."

I once witnessed this during a fitness challenge my friend decided to do. He was committed to running every day, and we planned his routine. However, it was a different story when he started to train and had to deal with days when he was too tired to move, when he got busy with other responsibilities, and even when he fell sick. He had made me his accountability partner, and sometimes I felt sorry for him when he would call and ask me to give him a pep talk as he got ready to keep to his routine even through great fatigue.

That's what it looks like to be constant. We must realize that despite our good feelings at the beginning of any project or a new phase of life, we will still go through tough times that test whether we meant what we said. Hardly anyone has achieved success without gritting their teeth and going through with it, no matter how they felt. When you set non-negotiable goals, you have to eliminate excuses. There is no place for "if I feel like it," only "I will do it."

One story that inspires me is that of J.K. Rowling. Before the success of *Harry Potter*, she faced rejection from 12 publishers, financial hardship as a single mother, and skepticism from nearly everyone around her. She had every reason to give up and walk away—but she chose to persevere. Because of that decision, *Harry Potter* has become one of the most successful and beloved book series in history. It has sold over 500 million copies worldwide, been translated into more than 80 languages, and spawned a multi-billion-dollar film franchise, theme parks, and a global fan base.

Perseverance isn't just about holding on—it's about the grit to keep going and the determination to stay the course, even when the road gets tough. It may require adjusting the parts of your goal that aren't working, but it never means saying, "I've failed too many times, so I'm done."

However, many times, we are unable to remain constant and true, despite our good intentions. I've discovered the psychology behind why that happens. People can stick to a goal and be consistent when they:

1. **Internalize the goal**: If the goal is tied to a personal aspiration or value, it becomes easier to fight to keep it. When they're not, it becomes easily discardable.
2. **Make the goal clear and specific:** Vague commitments like "I want to be healthier" are difficult to maintain. Specific goals like "I will exercise for 30 minutes daily" tell you exactly what you need to do.
3. **Seek accountability**: Sharing commitments with others creates a sense of responsibility because now somebody else is watching.
4. **Build habits around commitments:** When a goal becomes part of your routine, it's harder to abandon.
5. **Break down goals and celebrate small wins:** We get tired and fail to stay committed because we try to achieve the big things all at once. Instead, break the goal into smaller achievements and celebrate each level crossed.

Real, lasting constancy is built on purpose, clarity, and accountability. As a leader, I've had to inspire my team to stay constant by leading by example, getting them invested in the team's shared purpose and overall goal, and ensuring they have a say in the process to create ownership. Constancy turns intention into actual results and is the backbone of any change.

CHAPTER 5

Completion:
From Vision to Reality

"It does not matter how slowly you go as long as you do not stop." —Confucius

---

When Larry Page and Sergey Brin met at Stanford University, they soon realized that they had a common vision: to organize the world's information and make it universally accessible. The internet was growing rapidly, but finding relevant information was difficult. They believed they could create a better way—a search engine that ranked web pages based on relevance, not just keywords. In 1998, they launched Google from a small garage, facing skepticism from those who doubted its potential. At the time, search engines were cluttered and inefficient, but Page and Brin persisted, refining their algorithms and improving search accuracy. Their breakthrough was the PageRank algorithm, which revolutionized the way people accessed information online. Google's rise wasn't immediate. They faced technical challenges, funding struggles, and competition from established players. They'd conceived the vision, and they didn't stop until it became a reality. Google rapidly became the world's leading search engine, expanding into countless innovations, from Gmail and Google Maps to Artificial Intelligence.

The story of Larry Page and Sergey Brin illustrates the possibilities that can be realized if one has the fortitude to hold on until a process is complete. By refusing to settle for the status quo, they not only built a company but also changed the way the world interacts with information.

Every great endeavour is a marathon, not a sprint. Have you ever participated in a marathon? I will share a story that is common among most marathon runners. Like every daunting task, participating in a marathon starts as just an idea you have in your head. Every runner pictures themselves getting off the starting block, racing through the crowd of other runners, leaving many people behind as they lead the pack, then running through the finishing line, getting all the applause, and probably taking a trophy home. This is a vision common to all runners, whether the race is a marathon or a sprint. Everyone dreams of completing the race and succeeding at the end. The statistics, however, show the reality. According to statistics available to the public, the oldest and most prestigious marathon around the globe, the Boston Marathon, saw close to two hundred thousand applicants in 2024, and out of this large number, only a third (34%) completed the marathon. What happened to the larger percentage of the registered participants? This is what this chapter will address.

Only one individual emerges as the winner of every race, whether a one-hundred-metre Olympic competition or a leisurely marathon organized just for the fun of it. At most, the podium finishers in first, second, and third place are celebrated, while the others have to be consoled with the fact that they competed and completed. Yet, everyone who ran hoped they would clinch the winner's medal. Everyone saw a vision of themselves running through the finish line ahead of everyone else. And indeed, every marathon runner would have liked to complete the journey, but is it everyone who possesses the stamina to last through the long stretch? Certainly not. Let us take a look at what it takes to start something in life, and not just complete the task, but finish strong.

1. Conclusion: Crossing the Finish Line

There are a thousand reasons to quit, if you ask me. Yet, there are tens of thousands of reasons to finish. The decision lies with the individual. Do you want to be a champion or a loser? I've studied hundreds of biographies in my life, and I have found that there aren't many differences between the great achievers who changed the world and those who came to this Earth and left without affecting anyone throughout their existence. We are all made up of basically the same anatomy and heredity, but that's only part of the story. While we may share a common biological makeup, our circumstances vary widely. Some people are born into supportive environments with access to opportunities, while others face enormous obstacles from the very beginning. What separates us is the content of our minds—the things we believe, the thoughts and principles we live by, and what we know. Interestingly, most people want to live a life of some meaning; we want to do something for the world or our family. So why do we have such a small number of truly successful people? I spent a long time thinking about this question until the answer came to me. It is straightforward: most people start, only a few finish; and life rewards only finishers, not starters. As simple as this sounds, it is what distinguishes those whose lives became a strong force in the annals of history.

In four steps, let's examine the path that leads to a habit of concluding.

Celebrating Milestones: The Importance of Acknowledging Progress: I used to be someone who couldn't take my mind off the finish line. I was so preoccupied with lifting the trophy that I forgot how to enjoy the process that would take me there. You see, I soon realized that the human mind couldn't stay focused on one final success without achieving little successes along the way. If I refuse to allow my mind to enjoy that feeling of achievement for the little wins just because I want to wait for the one big final *hurrah*, my mind will not be able to build the fortitude I need to get to the end. The mind just doesn't work that way. It was when I learnt to enjoy my progress and celebrate my milestones that I became confident and strong enough to stay motivated for the big win. Acknowledging progress, no matter how little it seems, reminds us that we are on the path to success, and this is such a great catalyst to keep going till the end. Reward yourself, share your success story with other people, and keep track of your growth. These are the ways to keep your mind sharp until the finish line.

Learning from the Journey: Extracting Wisdom from the Process: One way I stay motivated until I arrive at the finish line is to enjoy the journey to the fullest and take away all the lessons that I can. The journey to the destination is just as important as the destination itself. Every action, mistake, decision, step, even the people I meet on the journey, everything teaches me something important for the entire journey. In practical terms, this is how I gain all the wisdom I can glean from the process that comes before the ultimate success:

1. I take some time to reflect every day, and I ask myself, *"What have I learnt?"* This ensures that I can assimilate all the lessons from both my mistakes and correct decisions for that day.
2. Rather than avoid challenges, I take them on and do my best to solve them because I know that each challenge helps me become stronger.
3. When a method doesn't work, I make a note of it and then I adjust, adapt, and improve. In this way, every step of the journey provides an opportunity to prepare for the destination.

The Art of Closure: Knowing When to Call It Done: I believe most of us have been here: You are working on a project, and you keep improving and adjusting things with the hope that you will get the perfect product before the deadline. However, you soon begin to realize that there is no way you can complete the assignment if you keep aiming for perfection. I've been like this often, especially during my student days. However, I soon learnt that it is good to always know when to bring something to an end. Closure is an ability everyone must possess to move forward to the next stage of life. This is how to demonstrate closure:

1. Set precise goals: This helps me to have a clear destination in mind and stop when I get there.
2. Don't overthink things: When a step is completed, rather than complicate it by tinkering with the methods, I move on to the next stage.
3. Prioritize progress rather than perfection: The question I

ask myself is simple: *"Did I improve over the last attempt?"* If *yes*, then I get closure even if I didn't attain perfection.

4. Appreciate the effort: I always take out time to commend myself for the task I have completed, then I let things go.
5. Let things go: Once a step is completed, whether it fails or succeeds, I recognize that I have finished that step, and I take all the lessons I can from that entire process before heading forward.

Redefining Success: Completion Vs. Perfection: When a team member joined my unit some years ago, due to the pressure he placed upon himself to impress me and the other leaders, he tried to pursue perfection. He didn't accept that anything was successful until he believed that it was perfect all around. He would spend hours and hours just trying to fine-tune every minute detail of a project that had been given the green light. He ended up wasting a lot of time and our unit resources on endless tweaks here and there. It got to a point that we, the leaders he was trying hard to impress, called him into a meeting and warned him to stop dragging back several projects. Team members also disliked working with him because he was needlessly breaking deadlines, just because of the new tweaks and changes he kept suggesting. I had to call this new member and teach him that the end goal of many projects was not perfection, but efficiency. This new philosophy changed his entire work outlook, and he started to become an effective, successful employee. Perfection has never been the goal. In all kinds of interactions and partnerships, it is important to note that relationships do not have to be perfect; they just need to be beneficial and bring happiness to both parties. Once we can redefine what success is, we will learn to focus on completion rather than chasing a perfect idea that may never come to reality.

2. Continuation: Beyond the Goal Post

It is not enough to gather people in an auditorium and give them an ultimatum that they must finish strong, that they must not quit, or that they must complete what they have started, when in reality, this is not an easy thing to do. How do you even get the desire to continue after you have arrived at the first bend of the marathon? What if you've completed several tasks and still find yourself stuck in one position? How do you continue even when you have completed half of the task?

Setting New Horizons: The Power of Continuous Improvement: I was one of those who used to think that arriving at a goal is the ultimate desire of a human mind, and that once that is achieved, there is no need to seek new adventures or travel any further. After I completed my graduate school, I quickly realized that no matter how high a target is, once it's been crossed, it becomes a piece of history. After I earned my degree, I was proud of my achievement. This feeling only lasted a few days before fading. I began to wonder: *"What's next?"* This was when I learnt that the most important part of every success story is not the finish line, but the progress and growth that happened along the way. Now, I focus on continuous improvement and set new goals after every great win. This has kept me motivated to keep going and growing. How do I achieve this?

a. I am always on the lookout for lessons to imbibe into my life as a new habit.

b. I embrace growth and live for improvement.

c. I ask for feedback after every major win.

d. I celebrate the progress, not just the result.

e. I set the new target higher than the last.

These steps keep me always on my toes and help me retain motivation.

Sustaining Momentum: Strategies for Long-Term Progress: Most relationships, just like a new business, start with many adrenaline rushes as both partners go through the first few weeks and months of the honeymoon period. Love is in the air, you think you can't live without the other person, and you want to see them every moment. However, in almost all cases, a few months later, everything dissipates, and the intense passion is lost. At this point, what sustains the relationship is the substance of friendship, habit, and mentality that the union has shared until that point. This also applies to startups. After a while, the short-term motivation fades, and we realize that it is not just about starting strong; there is a need to go all the way. How do I stay engaged and keep things on track?

1. I divide big goals into small, simple steps. This gives me a sense of confidence and helps me not to feel overwhelmed by the sheer enormity of my goals.
2. I create and stick to a routine to provide me with a structure and put in place good habits that will keep me going.
3. I keep reminding myself of the reasons why I started, particularly on tough days.
4. I keep track of my progress to keep myself on the right track. I create a checklist of milestones and reflect on the achievements.
5. I look for the big picture, the greater good, rather than focusing on the present, temporary difficulties, or pleasures. This helps me to stick it out for the long term.

The Continuation Mindset: Viewing Completion as a New Beginning: Once a task has been completed, this is the best time to chart the course for a new one. No fuel drives a new endeavour better than the sense of accomplishment that comes from completing a previous one. Even in things as simple as completing a novel or series, I see it as an opportunity to start a new one. Having this mentality helps one to consolidate the success achieved and pursue bigger things. Embracing a lifestyle of continuous work keeps me motivated to keep growing, and I do this by celebrating the end of a journey and the effort I put in to make it happen. Then, using the lessons I learnt from that concluded journey, I set new goals right away to retain momentum. By seeing every completed task or project as the start of something new, I am always open to new opportunities and a chance to start another cycle of growth.

Balancing Rest and Forward Motion: The Rhythm of Progress: I once spoke to a friend who confessed that if she wasn't doing anything, working on a current project, or pursuing a goal, he would feel as if he was regressing and start feeling like a failure. I had to speak to him for a long time and explain that progress is not about constant activity. One must know when to pause, refresh, and recharge before going again. Having a balance between taking a rest and running forward is key to long-term survival. Life isn't a sprint; you will need to rest in between stops, or else you may not have the stamina to last for the entire process. This is how I find the rhythm between moving forward and taking a rest:

1. I listen to my body and pay attention to my state of mind. When I realize that I'm worn out and tired, unable to

move on without difficulty, I simply take a rest without feeling guilty. The work I had put in when I was energized gives me the comfort and courage to relax, sleep, or go on a vacation if necessary, anything to ensure I am back to my best before continuing.

2. I set a very clear, deliberate schedule and stick to it. I have learnt that most people who become tired and give up along the way are not necessarily lazy; they are just people who do not respect the boundaries they had set. If you planned to close business by nine, please close by nine.

3. Even when taking a rest, I do it intentionally. I relax and take a break with the mindset of having a recharge and regard the time of rest as a part of my work process.

I distract my mind intermittently between tasks as a way to stay sharp and keep my mind refreshed. In most cases, I engage in hobbies that improve my overall efficiency, e.g, see a movie or watch some documentaries just to relax and refresh.

Since I found the balance between rest and work, I have managed to keep my energy optimal and my motivation consistent.

3. Culmination: The Peak of Achievement

It's a beautiful feeling to see everything you have worked for come together well. When it all works out, you look at what you have achieved with joy and a sense of fulfilment. To see that all your effort has culminated in something substantial … now that is a rewarding feeling! Knowing that life never stops, and the future is still far ahead, how do you manage this peak of achievement?

Recognizing Your Growth: Measuring Progress Beyond Metrics: I've spoken with many people who believe progress can only be measured by numbers—test scores, points earned, hours worked, report cards, or any other form of written achievement. If they don't hit the target metrics, they feel like they've failed. But I'm here to say that mindset doesn't capture the full picture.

True growth isn't defined by numbers alone. Real progress is about what changes within you—the lessons you've learned, the resilience you've built, and the mindset you've developed along the way. From my experience, adopting this broader view of growth brings a powerful shift in perspective. I've found myself working with more focus and long-term commitment, not just chasing validation through external results.

When you measure success purely through metrics, your effort often reflects a need for approval. But when you grow from the inside out, you begin to work with a deeper purpose. You're not trying to impress others—you're trying to improve yourself. And that shift changes everything about how you approach your goals, your work, and your life.

Leveraging Success for Future Endeavours: Each success you record in your life must be a source of pride to you, but this is not all. Apart from celebrating your wins, see each bit of progress as what it truly is - progress! This suggests that there is a next step that you have the opportunity to connect to. The confidence and lessons learnt from the completed work will catalyze your next project. I have made this my habit, and I always do my best to use one success story as a springboard for the next. Here's how I do this:

- I analyze my strengths and weaknesses to know what worked and what failed.
- I share my success story with my network and use this as a connection for new collaborations.
- Since I have recorded a success and my confidence is high, I set bolder targets.
- I embrace new opportunities even outside the field where I have succeeded.
- I don't allow too much time to pass between my last success and the next one.

I congratulate you on achieving so much; you deserve all the accolades, but that is not the end. Use this success to secure your future. That is how greatness grows.

The Summit Syndrome: Navigating Life After Big Achievements: When I passed the age of 30, I was overcome with mixed emotions. You see, I had always looked forward to that landmark age, and I had big dreams about getting to 30 years old in this world. To be fair to myself, I had made a lot of progress by that age and had taken many giant strides in my career and relationships. However, the question niggled in my mind, *"What now; what next?"* It was years later that I learnt that there is something called the "Summit Syndrome," a feeling of emptiness you feel when you reach the peak of your target or dream. Like a mountain, as you climb the summit and look down from that high point, you may be disappointed to realize that the view of the valleys and hills is not as satisfying as you'd envisaged. It happens this way in all areas of life. You have sacrificed a lot to pursue success, and now that you have attained it, you look back and wonder if it has all been worth it. The next question on your mind is just as heavy: "What *do I do next?*" This feeling can be so overwhelming that many people fall into depression and deep confusion when they achieve their big childhood dream. Here's how I manage this post-achievement emotion.

1. I acknowledge the feelings and process the emotions, accepting the fact that it is normal to feel uncertain, empty, and confused.
2. I remind myself of my journey's purpose by reading the long-term goals I had written down and reminding myself that I still have many other things to complete.
3. I simplify my big, long-term goals into smaller steps. This helps me to focus on growth and progress rather than achievement.
4. I speak to mentors and friends about my feelings and seek validation from my loved ones. This works almost every time.
5. I move on to the next project as quickly as I can.

Creating a Legacy: Ensuring Your Work Lives On: Your success should not end with you. Every substantial achievement must have the ability to live beyond the achiever, and it must be transmissible. This is why the best leaders are those who delegate and pass on their big successes to other people, and yet, the work continues. Steve Jobs did this so well with Apple that there was a strong structure in the organization that outlasted him. His story inspires me to always ask myself, "What *will be remembered about me?*" Full success is not defined in moments; it is about legacy, the generation that comes after. This is how I demonstrate a central focus of legacy in my life:

1. Always think in decades, long-term goals, and impact.
2. Teach and inspire others to take responsibility and make contributions.
3. Document the strategies and stories from the entire journey.
4. Be intentional in your decisions and choices, both big and small.
5. Live a life of impact and build for the future.

It is extremely fulfilling to know that your work will stay relevant regardless of your passing. This makes all your effort and sacrifices worth it.

4. Cohesion: Bringing It All Together

There are instances where I have worked on several projects at separate times within a year, and at the end of the calendar year, I realized that every project I had worked on had somehow been interconnected with the others. The results of a project were used as the hypothesis for the next, and the lessons of one served as the basic foundation for another. It is wonderful to see several parts of one's endeavours fitting into one another like a puzzle. Even if every part of the work does not link as cohesively as we want, we have to find a way to bring them all together. I like to think this is how life works, too. Your finances affect your dreams, your dreams affect your plans, your plans affect your relationships, your relationships affect your health, and your health, in turn, affects your finances. Everything is interconnected; the trick is knowing how to make decisions that positively benefit all the different parts of your life.

Integrating Lessons Learned: Synthesizing Knowledge into Wisdom: I have always enjoyed reading, so I gathered an immense amount of knowledge in my younger years. I picked up books on random topics, took courses on diverse fields, and sought knowledge wherever I could find it. Yet, it was when I began to take time to reflect on my personal experiences and beliefs that I began to have a better understanding. The first thing I understood was that knowledge is not wisdom, but it can be if I allow myself to internalize the things I have learnt. When I am at the crossroads of a major decision, my pool of knowledge is not what guides me; it is the experiences that help. This is how I turn knowledge into wisdom:

1. I reflect on past events and spend time analyzing past experiences so that I can know what to improve and take note of what is true.
2. I apply the knowledge I have gained to real-life scenarios and make decisions based on my judgment.
3. I compare my knowledge with others' and listen to different perspectives on the same subject matter. The accumulation and application of several knowledge banks synthesizes wisdom.
4. I trust myself and my decisions. If I have made a choice based on my available knowledge, then I have to show some confidence in that wisdom.

Synergizing Your Skills: Combining Abilities for Greater Impact: It can be confusing to possess several skills without getting the corresponding results. In most cases, when this happens, it is because the talented individual has been unable to combine the various skills into a confluence of efficiency. I was like too before I understood how these things work. I knew I had great communication skills, and I could do research quite well. Yet, I couldn't make excellent presentations. It wasn't until I learnt to combine my research skills and transmit them through communication that I began to make a name for myself as an excellent storyteller through presentations. I have found that it is immensely beneficial to be able to organize your skills and make them work together for greater impact, especially when the skills are complementary, such as creativity and problem-solving skills. Here are some other complementary skills: project management and innovation, strategy and teamwork, networking and people skills, writing and storytelling, and so many others. I am convinced that if we look inwards and reflect deeply enough, we can synergize our skills for more meaningful impact.

The Holistic Approach: Seeing the Forest and the Trees: There is a delicate balance that must be established here. The holistic approach is not just limited to seeing the big picture, though this is beneficial. It also entails not getting so carried away by the big picture that one forgets the fine individual details. Until I learnt to see both the forest (the big picture) and the trees (individual detail), I couldn't get to the peak of my development. I completed projects and got rewarded for them, but I lost a few team members along the way. Then, when I paid attention to collaboration and delegation, I couldn't meet targets. This was my story back then, despite having been a leader for a decade. I remember attending a conference where the holistic approach was taught, and I stepped back and considered my mode of work.

I realized that it was possible to find a balance between attention to detail and working for the greater good. This time of reflection changed everything for me, as I was then able to combine and compact the trees into a forest of efficiency. Here are the five tips I used to finally find the balance:

1. The overall goal must be clear and precise.
2. All smaller tasks must contribute to the actualization of this greater goal.
3. Immediate actions must take priority and be given full attention.
4. When necessary, adapt the smaller steps to enhance the bigger strategy, not the other way around.
5. Move forward quickly after completing individual tasks.

By adopting this approach, it has become easier to complete projects quickly and make headway with the fewest hitches. I highly recommend the trees and forest mindset to leaders.

Building Cohesive Teams and Organizations: This is an important piece of this chapter. I believe that companies, families, and organizations would record greater levels of success if only the members who make up these bodies were working on united fronts. In the history of mankind, of battles and wars, the victors are not always the most populous. There have been many cases where the bigger army was soundly defeated by a smaller unit of organized warriors. When cohesion and unity are lost within a team, and everyone works for themselves, the failure is often great. This is why I always recommend that leaders only accept people who are clear on their roles within the overall team and are committed to seeing the team succeed. How are great teams formed? How do you build a strong, cohesive team where everyone is aligned toward a common goal? I have some recommendations from my experience:

a. I encourage open communication by creating an environment where everyone feels safe enough to share ideas, give feedback, and air their opinion. We achieve this through meetings where everyone sits down and gets a chance to speak their mind. When communication is encouraged, team members feel a sense of belonging and work for the team.

b. I typically only accept team members whose individual goals align with the overall team objectives. When the specific goals of the individuals support the team's goals, it becomes easier to put great effort and time into making the team succeed.

c. I reward the team for every achievement, great or small, and I reward individuals for outstanding contributions. I ensure I do this openly to inspire others.

d. I prioritize collaboration in my teams and encourage knowledge sharing and mutual support. This builds trust and fosters respect amongst the members.

5. Certainty: The Final Push

Many high school students find it difficult to decide what to do after graduation. For those who don't continue to college, one of the main reasons—aside from financial limitations—is uncertainty about what path to take next. The confusion over whether to pursue the arts, sciences, or business often holds them back.

In contrast, students who had a clear idea of their goals—or whose parents had already mapped out a plan—were more likely to move forward smoothly. Even those who weren't particularly excited about college still managed to succeed simply because they weren't confused about their direction.

From my experience and observation, clarity of purpose is more valuable than enthusiasm. When you're unsure or indecisive, even a determined effort may not lead to success.

So, how do you find that clarity?

Overcoming Last-Minute Doubts: Strategies for the Home Stretch: It happens that people who have always been certain about their objectives can become uncertain when the project nears its end. "Will this work?" "Have I overlooked anything?" "What if I fail?" These are some of the questions that paralyze even the most capable in the final moments of their endeavour. These last-minute doubts usually cause me to fear and second-guess myself until I learnt to stay focused and embrace the questions and uncertainty as a part of the process. These are my strategies for finishing my race regardless of doubts that come in the dying minutes:

1. I choose to trust myself: I remind myself of the great accomplishments I have already made as part of the process, and then silence every voice of doubt. Sometimes, if it requires me to stand in front of a mirror and speak to myself to regain my confidence, I do it without hesitation. I have discovered that when voices

bring you fear, the best way to kill the fear is to speak to the fear with words of courage and faith. It works every time.

2. I catch my breath: Sometimes, doubts come in the last minute as a result of the overwhelming feeling of that comes with completing great works. There have been times when simply taking a break and pausing to calm myself before going for the final push does the trick. I have found that once my mind has rested, it regains clarity and becomes active again.

3. I simplify the final stages: If the concluding steps seem too intimidating for me to complete, and I find myself doubting if I have what it takes to take on tasks that look complicated, I write down the entire task and break it down into smaller, actionable steps. Simplifying the last steps into manageable action points gives me great confidence for the final push.

4. I collaborate and ask questions: I seek assistance and reassurance from others. I speak to friends and mentors about my doubts and gain confidence from their feedback and fresh perspective.

Sharpening Your Focus: Techniques for Certainty Under Pressure: Now and then, I have had to work under pressure and make decisions under overwhelming conditions. These were times when I had to think quickly and still manage to do things correctly and in order. Sometimes, our clarity and focus are tested by deadlines, extreme demands, or sheer stress. When this happens to me, I always remind myself to take some time to pause and think quickly. I learnt a three-way technique that is used by great war commanders during the height of battle: Pause, Rally,

& Visualize. First, they calm their nerves and meditate; it is when the pressure is greatest that men should not rush. Second, they gather their top captains and assign specific tasks to small teams. Finally, they rally their troops and tell them what success will look like. These techniques restore calm and keep focus sharp under threatening, high-pressure conditions.

Decision Making in the Eleventh Hour: When to Push Through or Pivot: I've found myself in situations where, despite multiple attempts, progress just wouldn't come. Each failure made me question whether I should stick to my original plan or try a completely different approach. This dilemma has come up many times, especially when leading major projects under tight deadlines. As the pressure builds and the deadline approaches, the choice becomes critical: should I stay the course or switch to an emergency plan? Over time, I've learned how to make that decision more confidently. The question I ask myself is: *What do I stand to lose or gain by continuing—or by changing direction?* I weigh the costs, evaluate potential outcomes, and consider the risks involved in both pushing forward and pivoting. By breaking things down this way, I usually reach a clearer decision about which path will most likely lead to success.

Communicating Certainty: Aligning Teams for the Final Push: It's one thing to be confident about your direction as a leader, but it's another to effectively communicate that clarity to your team, especially when things get tough. During high-pressure moments, such as looming deadlines and rising tension, team members may start looking for someone to blame. As a leader, you must stay calm and focused. This is when strong communication becomes essential.

Here's how I ensure clear communication, particularly during the final stages of a project:

1. Reinforce Roles and Responsibilities
   I consistently remind team members of their specific roles to prevent confusion and overlapping tasks. Clarity in responsibilities keeps things running smoothly.

2. Set Clear Priorities and Task Hierarchies
   In the rush to finish, it's easy for priorities to get mixed up. I make sure to communicate which tasks are most important and in what order they need to be tackled. This helps everyone stay aligned and focused.

3. Maintain Regular Check-ins Without Micromanaging
   During the final push, I check in regularly with team leads to monitor progress. It's important to clarify that this isn't micromanagement—instead, it's about offering timely reminders and conducting light audits to keep the team on track and motivated.

4. Keep the Team Focused on the Bigger Picture
   I remind everyone how their contributions fit into the overall goal. This perspective helps different teams stay united and work toward the same objective until the project is complete.

6. Contribution: Your Mark on the World

I truly believe that at the end of it all, when we have completed all the tasks and finished all the projects, when everything we set our hearts upon has been fulfilled, the greatest fulfilment is in the impact we have on all mankind, whether great or small. Think about it for a moment- if everyone who has ever walked upon the earth decides to leave something behind and make their mark positively in one way or the other, just think about how beautiful and easy the world would become for the next generations. Several giants of history were born in humbler conditions than you and I, and yet, they found a way to change the story of mankind positively. Abraham Lincoln made his mark, Florence Nightingale turned around human history for the better, and so did Alexander Fleming and Marie Curie. Regardless of creed, background, or field of work, I truly believe that the ability to make an indelible impact is inherent in every human being. I will prove this assertion in the subsequent paragraphs.

Assessing Your Impact: Measuring What Matters: There was a time when I was only focused on numbers and records. I looked at the quantity of work I had completed without considering the quality of life that had been improved by the work I'd done. I lived like this for the first five years of my professional life, but I always felt a deep emptiness anytime I began to count my accolades and prizes. It wasn't until I learnt to focus on what truly matters that I began to prioritize impact over numbers. The true essence of success is to impact our world on deeper levels. This is how I measure impact:

1. I focus on the impact of my goals on humanity instead of just ticking off tasks and projects completed. I always ask myself, *Who or what has been made better because of what I have done?*

2. I ask my community about how my work has impacted them. Rather than taking pride in success rates, completion statistics, or my income, I gather feedback from my clients about how my work has made life easier for them. This is a true assessment of impact.

3. I emphasize ethics and protect my values. Regardless of the temptation to substitute ethical values for quick profit, I prioritize doing the right thing always. There have been times when I have turned down opportunities due to my core values. If that is the only way I can show the world that to do the right thing, so be it.

4. I ensure that every task or project contributes to my personal development. Then, I coach others to do the same. This is the way I can contribute to my community's overall development.

5. Mentorship is always a great way to assess impact. I ask myself, *How many careers have I inspired because of the way I work?*

Paying It Forward: The Ripple Effect of Contribution: One way to make our mark in the world, and this is possibly the easiest method I employ, is to do good without expectations of any personal reward; just a charge to the recipient to pay it forward. I was given a lot of assistance from seniors when I was struggling through high school, and when I became a senior myself, I organized several free tutorial classes for junior students. At the end of my tutorials, I always encouraged the students to do the same for the next set of students. To date, whenever I visit the campus to give lectures or speeches, I check in with the students just to see if they still do this. Surprisingly, it has become a tradition in that department for senior students to give free classes to the junior students. We can never tell the impact of the little seed we sow in someone's life today. The seed of a good deed germinates and spreads further than we can imagine. This is the natural lifespan of every good deed - someone else reaps the fruits. By paying kindness forward, every one of us creates a ripple effect of goodness that not only benefits everyone else, but also has a way of bringing meaning and personal fulfilment to our own lives.

Finding Your Unique Way to Contribute: Aligning Skills with Needs: When it became clear to me that I needed to make a real difference in the world, some questions began to trouble my mind. I had some skill sets, but I wasn't quite sure how I would use them to improve other people's lives. I had to do a lot of reflecting and studying before I finally discovered that everyone has their unique way to contribute their quota. These are four ways I found my path.

1. I first had to identify where my strength lies. I also needed to know my passion; what inspires me, excites me, and what I wouldn't need any push to do. Once I recognized my areas of strength, I channeled my skill set into executing my passion.

2. I identified the need that was prevalent in my immediate community, and I was determined to close the gaps. With the skills and passion I had already become clear about, it was not difficult to start contributing my skills towards fulfilling the needs that people had around me.

3. I volunteered for greater causes. I was aware that I may not be able to stop a global issue like climate change, so what I did was contribute my skills to educating people about the human activities that cause this phenomenon.

By being a part of something bigger than myself, I found a way to improve human lives.

4. I collaborated a lot. I worked with people who had similar skills to mine, and together, we began to influence our community on a much larger scale.

These are the four ways everyone can find their path in life. As a general rule, nothing is too little to contribute.

The Contributor's Mindset: Shifting from Success to Significance: One thing I know for sure is that true success is beyond personal gains and achievements. The real achievement is seeing the relevance of your work in bringing ease and comfort to people, and the true gain entails making an impact and contributing to individuals' growth and development. This is the mindset of a contributor. It is paramount, and even necessary in the grand scheme of things, to empower others and help them succeed. This is the true purpose of being successful. When I started practising the contributor's mentality, I found that the striving for personal gains became secondary, and my great desire was to make a positive impact. was the most fulfilling feeling I'd ever experienced!

CHAPTER 6

Connection:
Weaving The Web of Success

"Realize that everything connects to everything else."
—Leonardo da Vinci

My career track led me to become Excelerate's CEO and Founder. Everything I ever studied, every job I ever did, and every institution I ever worked for all led me to the pinnacle of my profession as a coach and founder. It is all connected. I studied at MIT and Philadelphia University, and I spent over eight years as the Vice President for Enrollment Management and Marketing at the University of Dayton, and another seven years in a similar capacity at Northeastern University.

These years in education and management equipped me with the tools I needed to manage institutions and push for success on a global scale. And this is how I founded Excelerate. All the knowledge and structures I needed were acquired through the different parts of my journey to the present. They are all connected. All your decisions, actions, education, responsibilities, and journey are connected to weave the web of greatness you desire.

Billie Jean King didn't just dominate tennis—she transformed it. At a time when female athletes were undervalued and underpaid, she stood up for gender equality, often facing fierce resistance. Her most iconic moment came in 1973, when she defeated former men's champion Bobby Riggs in the globally televised "Battle of the Sexes," proving that women's tennis was just as competitive as men's and deserving of respect. Her fight didn't end there—she pushed for equal prize money, helping make the U.S. Open the first major tournament to offer equal pay, and co-founded the Women's Tennis Association to give female athletes a stronger voice. Every win, both on and off the court, contributed to her lasting legacy. By challenging the status quo, Billie Jean King paved the way for future generations to compete on equal terms.

1. Cooperation: The Power of Unity

No amount of talent or hard work will surpass or equate to unity. The way the world works, it is quite impossible for a single man to achieve the greatest feats. Go through history and take a look at all the greatest champions of industry, sports, or science who have ever worked on this Earth. Regardless of their genius, they had to work with several teams. The greatest CEOs are only great because they are excellent at choosing the right team for their business decisions; the best sportsmen surround themselves with coaches and staff who work hard to keep them fit and skilled; and even genius scientists work with laboratory assistants who help run experiments and analyses. There is power in unity, and you'll achieve far more together with other people than you will if working alone. However, it is harder to work together when cooperation is lacking among team members.

Building Win-Win Partnerships: Strategies for Mutual Success: I've worked with teams made up of individuals with diverse strengths and high levels of competence. One key lesson I quickly learned is that when strong personalities share a team, there's a real risk of conflict—unless everyone is aligned around a clear, common goal. Early on, I faced challenges collaborating with certain team members, but once we built trust and recognized the mutual benefits of partnership, everything changed. We shifted our mindset from competition to cooperation, and as a result, both individual performance and overall team success improved significantly. Here are the simple strategies I used to foster collaboration within the teams I've led:

1. I started by planning a way for everyone to benefit and achieve the same objective.
2. We maintained an open communication strategy to address all concerns efficiently.
3. Every team member offered value to other members by understanding their particular needs.
4. All members of the team need to cover for one another's lapses and build trust.
5. When the team wins, we take time to acknowledge efforts and celebrate both individual and team successes.

Collaborative Problem-Solving: Harnessing Collective Intelligence: We are all brilliant in our own right, but there's no greater wisdom than the kind that emerges when brilliant minds come together. One day, our boss walked into the office and offered a $5,000 prize to anyone who could develop a strategy to break into a region where our business had failed for the past ten years. Motivated by the reward and the recognition that came with it, each of us immediately set out to find a winning solution, working individually, driven by personal ambition. We had two days, but by the end of the first day, no one had come up with a viable plan. It became clear that our individual efforts were falling short. Realizing that the entire team would look bad if we failed, we shifted our focus from personal gain to protecting our shared reputation. Once we came together and collaborated, the solution that had eluded us for over 24 hours was developed in just two hours. In the end, the boss rewarded the whole team, and I walked away with a lasting lesson: there is tremendous power in collective problem-solving. Here's how we worked together to crack the problem:

1. Everyone was mandated to contribute at least one idea to solve the problem.
2. We appointed a leader to gather the ideas and record them.
3. We focused on diverse ideas and found a way to merge them.
4. We dissected and explored every idea by asking questions and finding answers to them.
5. We then selected the ideas that directly solve the problem with the least amount of time and resources.

The Prisoner's Dilemma: Lessons in Cooperation from Game Theory: There are always extreme situations where two individuals or teams would need to compete for limited resources. In the prisoner's dilemma theory, two persons separately arrested for a crime were given a choice to either cooperate for a reduced sentence or betray the other and be freed. Either both of them cooperate to have a moderately successful outcome, or each one focuses on getting a full profit for themself at the expense of the other. Through repeated experiments, it was concluded that the most beneficial decision was to cooperate and share the benefits, albeit half-and-half. By the rule of mathematical probability, the game theory concludes that cooperation will always provide better overall results than individual effort. Here are some lessons that this theory teaches about cooperation:

1. Always choose cooperation over competition.
2. Build trust in your partners; this will be helpful in the long run.
3. Focus on long-term advantages, not short-term.
4. Encourage open, honest communication.

Fostering a Culture of Cooperation in Competitive Environments: I have worked with people who prioritized individual achievements over team wins, and I have to tell you that these sorts of teams end up failing in the end. If that single bad apple is not removed from the team, the rest of the team members will become bogged down, and their efforts will be wasted. This happens every time, and this is why leaders must build a culture of cooperation even in places where competition thrives. This can be achieved by only rewarding team effort rather than individual effort, encouraging collaboration instead of comparison, and aligning team objectives with individual goals.

2. Closeness: Nurturing Key Relationships

When the chips are down, and we are exposed to the harsh realities of life, humans generally seek solace in the presence of other people. Neither the yachts nor the medals, awards, or bank accounts give as much comfort to the mind as human connections. All through his boxing career, Muhammad Ali was more than a boxer simply because he was a master at building and nurturing relationships. He met with presidents of nations, dined with industry leaders, and was a friend to TV and music stars. Have you ever wondered why he became known as the greatest boxer of all time? It is because his friends in high places repeated those words so often that it became widely accepted as the truth. In establishing greatness, relationships are crucial to the journey.

Building Your Inner Circle - Cultivating Deep, Meaningful Connections: Not everyone you meet will matter in your life, and certainly not everyone who becomes friends with you will become close to you. I had to recognize the truth in this statement before I could form beneficial relationships. Everyone may know a few things about me, but only a few will know everything about me. This is the meaning of a close circle. Networking is not all about exchanging contacts or business cards just to increase the mailing list; I had to learn this the hard way. Some years ago, I suffered a huge loss in my business and needed the help of people to support me to get back on my feet. I looked through my contacts without finding anyone to come to my aid. This was when I realized that it was important to make a distinction between acquaintances and true friends. It was only when I began to cultivate genuine, intentional relationships that I realized that connections are more about the quality than the quantity.

1. I am intentional about my connections; I ensure that we align in values and goals.
2. I invest my abilities, time, and substance in other people.

3. I show up when connections require my input, and I ensure that I add value.
4. I am vocal about appreciating people who are important to me.

The Strength of Weak Ties: Leveraging Your Extended Network: Though it is my inner circle that is closest to me and knows my worries and wins, the people whom I consider acquaintances or friends of friends have also contributed to my success, particularly in terms of referrals. There are some levels of greatness that one cannot attain just based on the influence of his immediate friends. There are situations where I have needed the connections of my secondary network to push a brand or product, and it was someone whom I had only met a few times who helped me with exactly what I needed. There are networks of people who are not particularly close to me but have offered access to fresh opportunities and new markets. We can tap into the advantages of 'weak ties' by steadily offering value, expanding connections, and respecting everyone. I have learned that if I consistently churn out value, it will not be difficult to leverage my networks.

Vulnerability in Leadership: The Power of Authentic Connections: What happens when you open up to your team about a personal challenge? Can a leader share stories of failure and struggle with those they lead? From my experience, one of the most powerful ways to build a connection with your team is by being honest about your human vulnerabilities. Initially, I was hesitant to be vulnerable—I feared it might make me appear weak. But to my surprise, it was in those moments of honesty that I earned the greatest respect from my team. When I shared my doubts and fears, it created a ripple effect: others began to open up, communication flowed more freely, and the overall dynamic of the team shifted. That experience taught me that showing vulnerability as a leader doesn't weaken your position—it strengthens the trust and bond within the team. After that turning point, several team members began sharing their own stories, and the culture of the team changed for the better. Authentic leadership fosters empathy, encourages openness, and builds a transparent environment where everyone feels supported. The result is a stronger, more collaborative team that is constantly improving together.

Balancing Professional and Personal Relationships: Striking the right balance between professionalism and personal connection can be tricky. Sometimes, we're too casual when we should be acting with professionalism, and at other times, we're too rigid when a friendly, personal touch is needed. Finding the right balance between the two often determines how successful our interactions and relationships will be. Early in my career, I struggled with this—misjudging situations and responding in ways that led to tension or even lost relationships. Over time, I learned how to navigate this balance more effectively. Here's what helped me:

- Communicate clearly: When I speak or write, I do it with clarity to prevent any misunderstandings from the other party. This has helped me to balance personal and professional relationships.
- Let the environment dictate: I try to provide context to my responses and behaviors, particularly in the workplace. Whether I am personal or professional usually depends on the situation at that moment in time. It is good to be aware of the surroundings, stakes, and persons involved before deciding how to behave.

- Respect privacy: It doesn't matter if you are my closest friend or a distant employee, I make it my responsibility to preserve your privacy and protect your information.

3. Compatibility: Finding Your Tribe

From my experience, what separates a close circle from a broader network is the natural compatibility I share with those who become part of my inner circle. I've noticed—and others I've spoken to have confirmed this—that we tend to gravitate toward people who align with our passions and values. This is where fulfillment begins. Instead of seeking acceptance from everyone, we're drawn to those who resonate with what matters most to us. Whether it's choosing a job, a workplace, a place to live, or even a life partner, it's always more rewarding in the long run to surround ourselves with people who belong to our "tribe." By tribe, I mean those who share our core values and ambitions. When that kind of compatibility exists, it's easier to be authentic, and our relationships become deeper and more meaningful.

Aligning Values in Business and Life: The Importance of Fit: I have received several invitations from institutions that I assumed had the same ambitions as I, and the relationship crashed simply because what determines compatibility in life and business is not ambition but values. It could be an invitation to speak or give a seminar, and it would get to a point where my value of being transparent and honest clashed with the top managers, who wanted us to play politics with some of the strategies we employed to attain more visibility. When you and your organization are not aligned in values, you will keep clashing and disagreeing. You'll become frustrated despite hitting all your milestones, and the company heads will waste a lot of time arguing with you about differences in values. This experience has taught me to prioritize values and beliefs whenever I look for opportunities. True, there are some values that I may be flexible about, but there are also core values that I believe represent who I am, and I do my best not to betray those values and lose myself. I have now learned to communicate my values clearly when seeking business partners and also align my ambitions with what I believe. In this way, I thrive and create a better working environment.

Creating Synergistic Teams with Complementary Skills and Personalities: I have worked in teams where everyone was gifted, but these gifts were all in the same areas. My team members were all creative people who found it easy to develop ideas and explore innovative ways to solve problems. While all the team members got along quite well, the team as a whole suffered so much that it had to be disbanded, and the members spread across other departments. The simple reason a compatible team of highly intelligent individuals failed is that everyone had ideas, but the team lacked practical, hardworkers who knew how to get things done. In the end, the team generated plenty of ideas with zero drive to execute them. The team had no real project manager to organize the ideas and make something out of them. As team leader, I had to take on several responsibilities in a bid to help out the team, and that took its toll on me, too. The funny thing is that once the team had been distributed across other units, their individual efficiency and appraisal shot up. These talented people had the ideas, but they needed people with different personalities to complement their skills. This is what is called 'synergy'. It is necessary to have diversity in thoughts and skills, and find a way to blend these different personalities into a smart team with collective strength and excellent collaboration.

The Diversity Advantage: Building Strength Through Differences: Beyond having diverse skills and talents, I've come to understand the immense value of building a team with a variety of cultural backgrounds, experiences, and strategic approaches. This kind of diversity becomes especially powerful when tackling complex challenges that require multiple perspectives to solve. When everyone on a team thinks the same way, creativity is limited, and that often leads to wasted time and stalled progress. In contrast, a team made up of individuals with different viewpoints can approach problems from various angles, leading to faster and more effective solutions. So, how do I build strength through diversity in background and personality?

1. I encourage open two-way communication where responses are provided to thoughts and questions shared, and everyone feels free to bring valuable strategies to the table, no matter how out-of-the-box those strategies sound.

2. I deliberately create a team by picking out people who are on opposite ends of the personality spectrum. By embracing this diversity from the point of recruitment, I make it clear to the team that I prefer it if everyone is different in some way. This helps every member of the team to feel accepted and appreciated.

3. I ensure that, though the individuals of the team are diverse, the goals are the same and success is team-based, not individual. By being clear about the team objectives, differences are used as an advantage to get results and keep the team growing.

When to Connect, When to Disconnect: Curating Your Network: In my early twenties, I struggled with the idea of letting people go. I believed I had to preserve every connection, fearing the discomfort and emotional pain that came with broken relationships. I even convinced myself that holding on to toxic relationships was a sign of emotional endurance. Over time, I learned that this mindset was holding me back. I had to accept that not everyone is meant to stay in my life—and that letting go is sometimes necessary for personal growth. Curating my network became one of the most valuable decisions I've made. It helped me become more intentional with my time and energy, and allowed me to focus on relationships that genuinely contributed to my productivity and growth. Here are the four steps I now use to curate my network:

1. I seek mutual value. We must help each other grow so that both of us bring something tangible to the relationship.
2. I pay more attention to the *quality* of people in my life rather than the *quantity*. This affords me more time to build deeper, meaningful connections with the few valuable people.
3. I am clear about the boundaries I have set for myself in terms of values and expectations, and I respect other people's boundaries too. This fosters mutual understanding and respect.
4. As I start to organize and create my network of close connections, I continue to stay open to more opportunities to meet more people who share common ambitions and personal principles. This is how I can disconnect with toxic time wasters and replenish my network without losing value.

4. Concern: The Glue of Relationships

As I've grown older, like most people, I've come to realize that life is full of both highs and lows. The highs are easy to enjoy— when things are going well, relationships feel strong, loyalty thrives, and everyone puts their best foot forward. But it's during the lows that true character is revealed. When resources are scarce, when failure feels close, and when others begin to doubt us—those are the moments that test the strength of our relationships. In those times, the friends who show genuine concern—the ones who offer support, empathy, and care regardless of the circumstances—stand out. Concern, in this sense, is more than just a feeling; it's an active trait that binds people together. It's what holds relationships steady through life's storms and challenges, making them resilient and enduring.

Long-term Thinking in a Short-term World: The Power of Loyalty: It is not always advisable to focus on quick wins, particularly in terms of relationships. I have learned to think about the long-term benefits, rather than what I would gain now. I have a childhood friend who used to squat with me in the room during my college days. The small room was uncomfortable for two of us, but I knew that I needed to help out a friend - that is just what friends do. Rather than focusing on the ease and comfort of staying alone in the room for those two years, I traded off the advantages to offer a helping hand to a friend. Well, as it turned out, ten years after college, my friend got a job with a leading business in the country, and he never forgot about the sacrifice I'd made for our friendship. In return, he recommended me for some of my biggest contracts when I started running

Excelerate. He was the one who referred me to his managers and helped me establish trust with his referrals. And this is just one single story; I have now realized that loyalty is crucial whether in business or personal relationships. You have to stay committed to people to build loyalty and reap the rewards of the connections you have established over time. Being consistent and reliable as a person makes it easy to show enough concern that can build a good foundation for future benefits.

Building Trust and Credibility over Time: There has always been the argument that the best things in life take time to form. Though many would disagree with the notion that time is an essential part of great relationships, I think that some things cannot be formed without the proper passage of time. Trust and credibility, for example, cannot be assured from the first day of a relationship or even the first year. I learned this the hard way when I used to trust every Tom, Dick, and Harry immediately I met them. After several betrayals, I quickly discovered that it was better for me to be careful of people until they had won my trust. Trust is built by continuous, repetitive consistency in character. And when trust is established, the personalities involved become credible enough for me to recommend them to others. These are four ways I build trust and credibility:

1. Whether in little assignments or enormous projects, I stay consistent with my quality of service. This is one of the best ways to build trust.
2. When I make a promise and give my word to people, I ensure that I follow it up with action, even if it comes at a personal cost. This helps me build credibility.
3. I do my best to do the right thing every single time. I know it is not always easy to do the most ethical thing and

uphold morals, but as much as I can, I try to make the right decisions.

4. I practice transparency in communications and actions. I avoid misunderstandings by being as open as I can. This has helped me to create a track record of honesty.

Concern in the Digital Age: Nurturing Relationships in a World of Options: I understand that times have changed, and information now flows endlessly through the palms of our hands and into our minds, mostly unfiltered. We have thousands of "friends" on the internet and tens of thousands of connections on social media. The overwhelming number of people that we have to keep up with often means that we have shallow interactions with everyone and no deep relationships with anyone. And is this not why loneliness has never been this high, especially amongst the younger generation? Without showing true concern for anyone through deep communication and compatibility of values, we can easily get distracted by the sheer number of people we need to keep up with. In a world where there are several options, we must be intentional about nurturing relationships and prioritizing values and people that truly matter. This is where intentional concern becomes vital. We have to spend quality time with people who share our values and learn to use technology as an *enhancer* of our relationships rather than an *inhibitor*. Visits should be done in person, and physical meetings should be planned now and then, instead of leaving everything to the easy method of technology.

The ROI of Relationship Investment: Why Concern in Connections Matter: In the end, almost everything we do—consciously or not—carries some benefit for us, and the same is true for building real, lasting connections. When we commit to relationships for the long term, we often see the rewards over time. Just like a financial investment that grows and pays off gradually, the return on investment (ROI) in relationships also takes time to mature. I've seen this firsthand. That friend I mentioned earlier, whom I gave a place to stay during college, returned the favor with an opportunity that came more than ten years later. That experience showed me that the trust and support we invest in people often come back to us in meaningful ways, sometimes long after we've forgotten about the effort. This isn't unique to me—it happens everywhere, especially in fields like politics, where people often benefit decades later from connections made early in their careers. That's why long-term, committed relationships matter. With patience, the benefits come—whether in the form of wise advice, valuable referrals, unexpected financial help, recommendations for influential positions, or simply a strong reputation and supportive network. These are the lasting profits of true friendship and meaningful connection.

5. Comfort: Creating Safe Spaces for Growth

At the centre of everything people do is a desire to be free to express ourselves without fear of judgment. In a study I was a part of, we sought to understand the greatest needs of young entrepreneurs. After security, one of the things people feel they most need to thrive is comfort. Young business owners want an environment that is comfortable for them to take risks and focus their attention on getting desired outcomes. Yes, I know that comfort can be an enabler of complacency, but it is also a fact that, as humans, we need to feel relaxed to put in our best efforts. Growth is not achieved in an environment filled with fear and a sense of insecurity.

Psychological Safety in Teams: Fostering an Environment of Trust: During my first year in the professional space, I attended several team meetings where people were too terrified of their boss for them to say anything useful. When the leader asked a question, we all kept quiet and refused to contribute our ideas. Because this team leader was a self-absorbed person, she never bothered to ask us why we kept mute in most of the meetings. I had even started to think that this was probably the norm in every workplace until I was transferred to another unit and saw how the team members spoke up and felt safe enough to offer their opinion on key decisions. The differences between this new team and the former one were quite huge. The team output was far greater in the new team, the collaboration was far more efficient, and more people applied to join this new unit. The previous team didn't survive another business year before it collapsed into another unit. I am convinced that leaders must always prioritize open communication and an atmosphere of comfort and safety. This kind of space gives people room to take more risks and brainstorm on proposing solutions without fear of being judged or criticized. When members of a team aren't afraid to make mistakes, it is easier to coach and improve the team and help them innovate for success.

Balancing Challenge and Support: The Growth-Comfort Paradox: There have been situations where I have seen people being so supported and assisted that they become overly dependent on their team leaders. Too much comfort leads to complacency. When, rather than allow a bird to fly, we keep holding its wings and pushing it through the air, such a bird may end up never learning how to fly. Challenging people and allowing them to fail on their own, on the other hand, can become so extreme that they lose every iota of confidence they have, and this will also negatively impact their growth. Stagnation is the result of too much comfort, while loss of confidence happens when people become too pushed. Finding the right balance between both extremes gives people the best support. I have learned to push people out of their comfort zone, but still stay with them to offer a hand when they do things that are beyond their scope. The trick is to set realistic challenges that will stretch people's abilities and still be available to advise, but not take over their tasks. This is the way to build comfortable growth.

Creating Comfort in Uncomfortable Situations: Techniques for Ease: What if I'm suddenly thrown into a difficult situation—forced to face a challenge alone, without support, or asked a question I don't know how to answer? What do I do then? Life will inevitably present us with uncomfortable and uncertain moments, and learning how to handle them is essential. From my experience, growth often comes when we push through discomfort and find a way forward. Think back to the first time you asked someone out on a date—it probably wasn't easy or comfortable. But you did it, and chances are, you gained something valuable from the experience. The same applies to other challenging moments. When we learn to manage the doubt and anxiety that come with discomfort, we become better prepared to navigate the world with confidence. Here are a few techniques I use to handle such situations:

1. I breathe and focus on the objective, not the unfavourable conditions.
2. I start with the easiest task, begin with the first step, and then take the next.
3. I think about what I stand to gain, not what I could lose.
4. Preparation gives confidence; practice makes perfect.
5. I ask questions when in doubt and listen to the other party.
6. I boost my confidence with tasks I am competent in and spend more time on them.

Whether giving a speech at a conference, speaking with someone I like, or standing before a senate hearing, these tips have proven to be highly effective in creating ease in the most uncomfortable conditions.

The Comfort Zone Trap: When Comfort Hinders Growth: I've often found myself feeling stuck in jobs that didn't challenge me, even when the pay was good. And I know I'm not alone. When every task becomes too predictable, every outcome the same, and the path to a solution is always straightforward, the mind begins to stagnate, and personal growth slows down. Psychologically, it's well-established that challenge and innovation drive positive growth. Without them, stagnation sets in, and over time, it can lead to redundancy or even regression. Skills we've worked hard to acquire can become outdated, techniques fade, and our mental sharpness begins to dull. Staying too long in a role without risk or difficulty doesn't just limit personal development; it can also negatively affect your career by keeping you from embracing bigger, more meaningful opportunities. To avoid falling into this rut, I've developed a few strategies that help me stay engaged and growing, even in seemingly comfortable roles:

1. I acknowledge when I am too comfortable and recognize the need to evolve.
2. I seek new hobbies and volunteering roles in a way to inspire creativity and keep myself motivated.
3. If hobbies don't help, I go all out to seek new opportunities despite the possibility of failure.
4. I take risks in a bid to provoke some spark inside me and gradually get myself out of my comfort zone.
5. I generally don't allow myself to stay too long in a space before seeking greater challenges; I am comfortable with being uncomfortable.

6. Consideration: The Art of Thoughtfulness

It seems fitting to me that this is one of the very last points in this book. There are simple, kind gestures and little acts of compassion that resonate so much with the human soul that everyone feels blessed to receive such gifts. To have someone hold a door for you as they go through, to see a car slow down on a busy road just so people can cross, to have someone warmly lay an arm on your shoulder when you are grieving a loss, to leave a last slice of cake for a friend who is out, and to remember a person's birthday and give them a call - these are simple acts of consideration that shows deep thoughtfulness and kindness. These acts do not require much intense labour or sacrifice on the part of the giver, but they always mean the world to the recipient. I strongly believe that if the world can embody more thoughtfulness and be a little more considerate, the entire human race will greatly benefit and improve.

Small Gestures, Big Impact: The Power of Micro-Considerations: I've been there too—completely defeated. I had just lost a major contract, and the weight of that failure sat heavily on my shoulders. It wasn't just a personal loss; it was a blow to my entire team, and I felt responsible. That day had been one of the worst, and as I sat alone on a park bench with a coffee in hand, I found myself questioning everything. While I was lost in thought, a little girl no older than six or seven caught my attention. She was laughing, carefree, playing with two balloons tied to long strings. For reasons I'll never know, she walked up to me and handed me one of the balloons, smiling brightly. Her joy was contagious, and even though I felt broken inside, I couldn't say no. I stood beside her, watching the balloons float gently in the breeze. A few minutes later, her mother called her away. She left one of the balloons with me, skipping off without a word. That small act of kindness turned everything around. It wasn't about the balloon—it was about the moment. That simple gesture brought light into my darkest day, lifting my spirits and restoring a sense of hope. The following Monday, with renewed confidence, I approached a new client and landed the biggest account of my career. As congratulations poured in and my bosses praised my work, I knew the turning point wasn't just strategy or luck—it was that little girl's kindness. This is the power of small gestures. You never know how deeply a simple act of thoughtfulness can impact someone. Micro-considerations may seem insignificant, but they can create a ripple effect that changes everything.

Cultivating Empathy in Leadership: Seeing Through Others' Eyes: There are some things you only learn when you lead a team, and for me, it was empathy. I always thought that I could understand how people felt just because I was compassionate and could understand their plight. However, it was only when I became a leader of a large team that I began to learn what true empathy entails. Rather than focusing on results, tasks, and outcomes, I needed to learn how to understand the emotion behind decisions, personal limitations, and individual shortcomings. This was when I started to cultivate empathy by looking at things through other people's eyes. Once I became quite good at being empathetic, my leadership assessment rose, and team members always had a good word to say about me. This is how I practice empathy in leadership:

1. I listen actively with genuine interest and encourage people to share their personal stories.
2. I appreciate people easily and frequently, giving them a sense of acknowledgement.
3. I offer support and help get tasks done whenever there is a shortage of manpower.
4. I ask questions and seek understanding before I pass judgment or give feedback.
5. I share my experiences with the team and encourage them to do the same.

Cultural Consideration: Navigating Global Relationships with Grace: Being considerate of other people's cultural differences and personal preferences is a great way to show kindness and thoughtfulness. I have been in multinational meetings where people were forced to eat the same thing, drink the same way, and even sit in the same specific order and manner. These meetings were largely redundant and unproductive simply because several participants felt offended or ignored by the institution's insistence to serve some types of foods and drinks without being considerate of people who were from another culture. If we intend to run a global market, then we must embrace a global mindset in our dealings. How do I navigate global relationships to demonstrate cultural consideration?

1. I constantly educate myself on cultural norms, etiquette, values, and nuances. By asking questions and seeking to understand certain behaviors, I have been able to forge real relationships across nationalities.
2. I observe people and listen to cues and words. By paying attention to people's peculiar preferences, I have learned a lot about cultural lifestyles, and this has helped me to build relationships with total strangers within a short time.
3. I show respect to diversity and differences by acknowledging diverse tastes without enforcing mine or regarding my preferences as the better choice.
4. I am flexible enough to adapt my approach and business methods to fit into the culture of the area where I find myself.

The Considerate Communicator: Enhancing Connections Through Thoughtful Interactions: It's common in relationships for one person to talk too much without listening, and I've been guilty of this myself. It wasn't that I didn't care about my partner's perspective; I was just too caught up in my thoughts to realize that real communication is a two-way street. I often spoke too quickly, too harshly, or for too long, jumping from one point to another without giving the other person time to absorb what I was saying. I rarely paused for feedback, and I didn't consider how my words might make others feel. In those early years, I took pride in being someone who always "spoke the truth," but I didn't realize that the way I delivered my truth was hurting my relationships. Even as I began to lose connection with people close to me, I failed to reflect on how my communication style contributed to the distance. Eventually, things became so bad that when I started talking, people would simply nod and walk away. That was the moment I had to ask myself: What have I become? I've since learned that words carry weight, and those who speak must take full responsibility—not just for what they say, but also for how they say it. Tone, timing, delivery, intention, and even body language all matter. Thoughtful communication requires awareness and care. Here are seven markers of mindful and respectful communication:

1. I am intentional about both verbal and non-verbal expressions.
2. When I say it, it means I mean it. I don't say things that I do not mean.
3. I speak audibly and clearly, even if in a whisper or a soft voice.
4. I consider other people's perspectives through active listening
5. I ask for feedback and wait for a response when I talk for a long time
6. I give context to information, particularly when it is easy to be misunderstood.
7. I do not speak over other people's voices; I speak with them.

Through considerate communication, a lot is achieved and success is won.

Charting Your Course to Sea Change

Synthesizing the 36 'C's: Your Personal Transformation Roadmap

Throughout my journey of self-improvement and personal development, I have learned that a strong character is not just about good intentions. It often needs to be followed up with consistent, deliberate decisions that are in agreement with the values I represent. I believe that if we are all committed to the concept of atomic habits, of small steps to great decisions, and impact made in simple things, we will all arrive at a positive destination. This is the basis of all the 36 values or ideas that I have shared in this book. These 36 behaviors represent segments of a large framework that shapes a person's character. Whether it is courage, consideration, or communication, each habit provides a plan on what steps to take to become the very best version of myself every day. I have lived through these values, and my life has been changed by them as I have improved my mentality, habits, and relationships.

Setting these C tenets as the foundations of my life has also helped me become more relevant to my community, and I have grown as a more confident and competent leader. These behaviours are found in all the greatest men who have ever walked the Earth, and I strive every day to ensure that they become my second nature as I continue to evolve. The journey has been difficult sometimes, with some days easy and some hard, but I have decided to never give up until I become the best I can be, and so should you.

The Compound Effect: How Small 'C' Changes Create Massive Impact

One thing I quickly learned, and which I must emphasize, is that the transformations we make in our lives are not going to happen overnight. Big results are not achieved at the speed of light, but by a deliberate set of action plans. I am a strong proponent of getting great things done through small, organized decisions and actions. It is the consistent application of these C values that will multiply into transgenerational evolution and extraordinary impact. Each day, at the crack of dawn, and as I stand from my bed, I resolve to imbibe the character of the positive Cs into my daily tasks and interactions, and the next day, I repeat this same resolution. Though these changes will seem insignificant at first, by being committed to the course of action, sticking to my decisions every day, I have been able to create a compound momentum that is now so profound that I can no longer go back to the way things used to be. The results have been massive, leading to a life of positive growth that is both sustainable and natural.

Rather than expecting everything to change all at once or waiting for an extraordinary, dramatic shift in the way I used to be, I decided to trust the process and play the long game. Just by focusing on the right choice at every opportunity that I get, I have been able to accumulate the small steps and positive minor improvements into a complete change in my life. However, it took a long time of dedication to the course before these changes became my habits. And this is what I must emphasize here. Think of this as a long journey, rather than a short sprint. There is much power and beauty in consistent progress.

Your Invitation to Continuous Growth: The Never-Ending Sea Change Journey

Though I have described this growth process as a long journey, I am aware that there is no destination. No landmark would signify a final arrival into a position where everything is now all perfect - no, this is a journey of a lifetime, and you and I will keep going until we conclude our lives. Every moment, every mistake, every decision, and every victory that happens on the journey contributes to the growth and is indeed the growth. The key is to focus on the experiences that create additional value to the journey and learn from the setbacks. These obstacles and challenges are opportunities to learn, adapt, and improve in the areas of limitation while consolidating on the positive changes for continuous, uninterrupted growth, like a never-ending sea of change.

Start your journey today.
Start with the first change.
Start with the smallest step.
Start small, start little, or start alone, but start nonetheless.
This is my invitation to you.

Your C-Change Toolkit

Self-Assessment Questionnaires: Mapping Your 'C' Strengths and Growth Areas

It is necessary to regularly check in with yourself as you go through this journey. This will help you know your strengths and identify the areas of improvement. In this segment, you are required to make a list of a series of questions that will help you track your progress with the 36 behaviors and keep you in check. I recommend approaching this exercise with honest, even harsh feedback, and moving forward with renewed strength. This self-assessment is for you to gain clarity, not to judge yourself for having done well or not.

These are questions to reflect upon. Get a notepad to track your responses.

1. Courage: Facing the Storm

- Do I take action despite fear, or do I let fear hold me back?
- When faced with challenges, do I push through rather than avoid them?
- Do I stand up for what I believe in, even when it's unpopular or difficult?

2. Compassion: The Heart of Leadership

- Do I genuinely listen to and empathize with others' struggles?
- Am I willing to help others, even when there's nothing in it for me?
- Do I treat people with kindness, even when I'm stressed or frustrated?

3. Consistency: The Silent Power

- Do I follow through on my commitments, even when motivation fades?
- Am I reliable in my actions, words, and decisions over time?
- Do I stick to positive habits and routines, even when progress feels slow?

4. Conscience: Your Moral Anchor

- Do I make decisions based on my core values, even when it's difficult?
- Am I honest with myself and others, even when no one is watching?
- Do I feel at peace with my choices, knowing they align with what is right?

5. Courtesy: The Art of Respect

- Do I treat everyone with respect, regardless of status or background?
- Am I mindful of how my words and actions affect others?

- Do I practice gratitude, politeness, and good manners in daily interactions?

6. Commitment: The Fuel for Success

- Do I stay dedicated to my goals, even when obstacles arise?
- Am I willing to put in consistent effort, rather than seeking shortcuts?
- Do I honor my promises and responsibilities, even when it's inconvenient?

7. Curiosity: The Fuel for Evolution

- Do I actively seek out new knowledge and experiences, even outside my comfort zone?
- When faced with something unfamiliar, do I ask questions and explore rather than dismiss it?
- Do I challenge my own beliefs and assumptions to grow intellectually?

8. Create: Turning Ideas into Reality

- Do I regularly engage in activities that allow me to express creativity, such as writing, art, or problem-solving?
- When I encounter a problem, do I look for innovative solutions rather than defaulting to conventional approaches?
- Do I give myself permission to experiment and fail in the creative process?

9. Craft: Honing Your Skills

- Do I take pride in refining my skills and producing high-quality work?
- Am I willing to invest time in mastering the details of my craft, even when no one is watching?
- Do I seek feedback to improve my skills rather than settling for mediocrity?

10. Cognition: Sharpening Your Mental Edge

- Do I make time for deep thinking and reflection in my daily life?
- Am I able to analyze situations logically and make informed decisions based on evidence?
- Do I actively work on improving my memory, focus, and problem-solving abilities?

11. Consolidation: Building Your Legacy

- Am I bringing new ideas, projects, or solutions into existence regularly?
- Do I think long-term in my creations rather than immediate profits?
- Do I stay true to paths that will be relevant to the upcoming generation?

12. Conception: Birth of New Possibilities

- Can I generate fresh ideas and envision possibilities before others see them?
- Do I take the time to map out and develop my ideas into actionable plans?

- Do I encourage open-minded thinking and allow ideas to evolve organically?

13. Clarity: Cutting Through the Noise

- Do I clearly define my goals and priorities to avoid distractions?
- When communicating, do I express my thoughts concisely and effectively?
- Do I seek clarity in complex situations instead of remaining confused or uncertain?

14. Collaboration: Synergy in Action

- Do I work well with others by listening, contributing, and respecting different perspectives?
- Am I open to feedback and willing to adjust my approach for the benefit of the team?
- Do I recognize and leverage the strengths of others to achieve a common goal?

15. Connection: The Human Touch in a Digital World

- Do I make an effort to build meaningful relationships rather than just surface-level interactions?
- Am I fully present when engaging with others, rather than being distracted by technology?
- Do I show empathy and genuine interest in others' experiences and perspectives?

16. Consensus: The Art of Agreement

- Do I seek to understand different viewpoints before making decisions?

- Am I willing to compromise and find common ground when conflicts arise?
- Do I facilitate constructive discussions to help others reach agreements?

17. Conveyance: Mastering the Message

- Do I communicate my ideas clearly and effectively to different audiences?
- Am I aware of how my tone, body language, and choice of words impact my message?
- Do I actively seek to improve my ability to influence and inspire others through communication?

18. Charisma: Inspiring Others to Action

- Do I make others feel valued and motivated when they interact with me?
- Am I able to captivate and engage people with my energy and enthusiasm?
- Do I inspire confidence in others through my authenticity and presence?

19. Challenge: Embracing the Uncomfortable

- Do I actively seek out challenges to grow rather than avoiding difficult situations?
- When faced with discomfort, do I push forward rather than retreat?
- Do I view setbacks as learning opportunities instead of failures?

20. Catalyst: Sparking Transformation

- Do I inspire and encourage others to make positive changes in their lives?
- Am I proactive in driving change instead of waiting for circumstances to shift?
- Do I embrace opportunities to disrupt the status quo for the better?

21. Conviction: Unwavering in the Face of Doubt

- Do I stand by my values and beliefs even when faced with opposition?
- Can I make decisions confidently without excessive second-guessing?
- Do I remain committed to my goals despite obstacles and criticism?

22. Circumstance: Mastering Any Situation

- Do I adapt quickly to changes and unexpected challenges?
- Am I able to maintain composure and think clearly under pressure?
- Do I find ways to turn difficult situations into opportunities?

23. Contemplation: The Fuel of Evolution

- Do I take the extra step to find out the inner workings of ideas?
- Am I interested in learning how things work and asking why?

- Do I follow up on questions and explore new solutions until a problem is solved?

24. Constancy: The Backbone of Change

- Do I follow through on my promises and responsibilities?
- Am I willing to put in consistent effort even when motivation fades?
- Do I remain dedicated to my long-term goals despite difficulties?

25. Conclusion: Crossing the Finish Line

- Do I complete tasks and projects instead of leaving them unfinished?
- Am I able to push through the final stretch even when I feel exhausted?
- Do I celebrate my achievements and reflect on lessons learned after completing something?

26. Continuation: Beyond the Goal Post

- Do I seek continuous improvement even after reaching a milestone?
- Am I willing to set new challenges for myself rather than becoming complacent?
- Do I apply past lessons to future endeavors to ensure ongoing growth?

27. Culmination: The Peak of Achievement

- Do I strive to reach the highest level of success in my field or pursuits?

- Am I able to recognize when I've reached a major accomplishment and take pride in it?
- Do I use my achievements to inspire and uplift others?

28. Cohesion: Bringing It All Together

- Do I integrate different aspects of my life in a way that creates balance and harmony?
- Am I able to unify diverse ideas and perspectives to create a cohesive whole?
- Do I build strong, supportive networks that reinforce my goals and values?

29. Certainty: The Final Push

- How often do I work on having a clear objective in mind in the face of challenges?
- Do I remain true to my motive and goal even when distractions are numerous?
- Have I been able to achieve a mindset that does not take criticisms too personally?

30. Contribution: Your Mark on the World

- Am I making a positive impact on others through my actions and efforts?
- Do I share my knowledge and resources to uplift those around me?
- Am I leaving a lasting legacy that reflects my values and purpose?

31. Cooperation: The Power of Unity

- Do I willingly collaborate with others instead of insisting on doing things alone?
- Am I able to navigate disagreements and work towards shared solutions?
- Do I recognize the strengths and contributions of my team members?

32. Closeness: Nurturing Key Relationships

- Do I actively maintain and strengthen my relationships with those who matter most?
- Am I intentional about spending quality time with loved ones?
- Do I express appreciation and gratitude for the people in my life?

33. Compatibility: Finding Your Tribe

- Do I surround myself with people who align with my values and aspirations?
- Am I able to identify and build connections with those who truly support my growth?
- Do I recognize when relationships are not serving me and adjust accordingly?

34. Concern: The Glue of Relationships

- Do I show loyalty and dedication to my close relationships?
- Am I willing to work through difficulties instead of giving up too easily?

- Do I make consistent efforts to nurture and improve my relationships?

35. Comfort: Creating Safe Spaces for Growth

- Do I provide a judgment-free space where others feel safe to be themselves?
- Am I able to create an environment where people feel heard and valued?
- Do I offer support and reassurance when others are facing challenges?

36. Consideration: The Art of Thoughtfulness

- Do I take the time to understand and consider other people's perspectives?
- Am I intentional about showing kindness and generosity in my daily interactions?
- Do I anticipate the needs of others and act with empathy?

I recommend that you create a personal roadmap based on your responses to each question and design a tracker to help you improve on areas of limitation.

ACTION PLAN TEMPLATES: TURNING INSIGHTS INTO CONCRETE STEPS

Your responses to the self-assessment questionnaires should help you convert what you have learned about yourself into clear, practicable improvement goals. These templates will help you to set specific timelines, plan a course of action, and decide the metrics to grade progress.

Action Plan Template for _____ [Behavior Name]:

Goal: What specific change or improvement do I want to make related to this behavior?

Example: I want to increase my consistency in following through on commitments, especially with my team.

1.

2.

Action Steps: What specific actions will I take to achieve this goal?

Example:

1. Review my calendar each morning and set clear priorities for the day.
2. Break larger tasks into smaller, manageable pieces to avoid overwhelm.
3. Set reminders to ensure follow-up on all tasks.

Timeline: What is my target date for completing this goal, and what smaller milestones will I set along the way?

Example:

1. Start tracking my daily priorities immediately.
2. By the end of week one, review my progress and adjust if needed.
3. By the end of the month, evaluate my consistency and note any improvements.

Challenges and Solutions: What potential obstacles might I encounter, and how can I address them?

Example:

1. Challenge: Procrastination when faced with tasks that feel overwhelming.
2. Solution: Break tasks into smaller steps and tackle one thing at a time to build momentum.

Metrics for Success: How will I measure my progress?

Example:

1. Track the number of times I meet my daily priorities versus the number of times I fall behind.
2. Collect feedback from my team to see if they notice increased follow-through on commitments.

This template can be replicated for each of your areas of improvement with intention and consistency.

Reflection Exercises: Deepening Your Understanding and Application of the Cs

Reflection is necessary to improve your personal growth. Find time to reflect on your area of C improvement at the end of each day. Be honest and compassionate with yourself as you reflect on what you might have missed or where you might have defaulted during the day's activities. Remember, reflection is for you to grow, not to be perfect.

Reflection Exercise 1: Identifying Patterns in Your Behavior

1. Which of the 'C' behaviors do I naturally excel at, and why do I think that is?
2. Which of the 'C' behaviors do I find most challenging, and what do I believe is holding me back from fully embracing them?
3. Can I identify any patterns in my behavior when I face challenges or stress? How do these patterns reflect the 'C' behaviors I'm working to strengthen?
4. What past experiences have shaped my current approach to these behaviors?

Reflection Exercise 2: Looking Back to Move Forward

1. Reflect on a time when you successfully embodied one of the 'C' behaviors. What did it feel like, and what were the results?
2. Think about a recent situation where you struggled to demonstrate a specific 'C' behavior. What did you learn from this experience, and how can you approach it differently next time?

3. How does embodying these 'C' behaviors impact my relationships with others? Can I think of a specific example where a certain behavior created a positive connection?

Reflection Exercise 3: Vision for Future Growth

1. How do I want to evolve in the next six months in relation to these behaviors?
2. What specific actions can I take to improve the behaviors that need more focus?
3. How will I celebrate my progress along the way?

By engaging in these reflection exercises regularly, you will develop each of these C habits with little consistent effort.